Praise for previous editions of
Mac OS X Pocket Guide

"It doesn't matter what your computer skill level is, this handbook will show you what you need to get moving in the Mac OS X fast lane."

— Sean Alexandre, Bishop Eastern Sierra Macintosh User Group

"A very good roadmap through the latest version of the Mac operating system.... I highly recommend it for your reference library. With its small size you can easily keep it on your desk, or slip it in a desk drawer."

— Rodney Broder, Mactechnics

"The book is richly illustrated, replete with tables, screen shots, hints and illustrations. These allow you to determine what/how to do in OS X the many tasks that were once 'routine and easy' from whatever system you've switched from. The 150 page 'Pocket-Guide' level book provides a straight-to-the-point 'primer' on working Mac OS X. This well written, exhaustively indexed, little guide book is highly recommended to anyone who is about to or recently switched to Mac OS X."

— Harry (doc) Babad, *maccompanion.com*

"These mini Pocket Guides from O'Reilly answer almost all the essential questions.... Anyone with even minimal experience at Mac OS systems, old or new, will be using these handy guides often.... [Toporek's] got about 10 pages on basic Unix commands, for example, a subject I always start to glaze over when it comes up. But he gives the skinny with a clarity I could understand, and now I'm practically ready to be a superuser."

— Stephen M.H. Braitman, BOOK BYTES

Mac OS X Tiger
Pocket Guide

Mac OS X Tiger
Pocket Guide

Chuck Toporek

O'REILLY®

Beijing · Cambridge · Farnham · Köln · Paris · Sebastopol · Taipei · Tokyo

Mac OS X Tiger Pocket Guide
by Chuck Toporek

Copyright © 2005, 2004, 2003, 2002 O'Reilly Media, Inc. Previous editions of this book were published under the titles *Mac OS X Pocket Reference*, *Mac OS X Pocket Guide*, and *Mac OS X Panther Pocket Guide*. All rights reserved. Printed in the United States of America.

Published by O'Reilly Media, Inc., 1005 Gravenstein Highway North, Sebastopol, CA 95472.

O'Reilly books may be purchased for educational, business, or sales promotional use. Online editions are also available for most titles (*safari.oreilly.com*). For more information, contact our corporate/institutional sales department: (800) 998-9938 or *corporate@oreilly.com*.

Editor:	Chuck Toporek
Production Editors:	Claire Cloutier and Darren Kelly
Cover Designer:	Emma Colby
Interior Designer:	David Futato

Printing History:

May 2002:	First Edition.
November 2002:	Second Edition.
November 2003:	Third Edition.
June 2005:	Fourth Edition.

0-596-00914-3
[C]

Contents

Part III. Mac OS X Basics

Part IV. System Preferences

Part V. Applications and Utilities

Introduction

For the past few years, Apple has been chugging along hard and fast, revving Mac OS X at a pace nearly as fast as some of the big cats it's named for can move through the jungle. If you've been with Mac OS X from the start, you've seen Puma, Cheetah, Jaguar, and Panther, and now we're at the next big kitty: Mac OS X Tiger (Version 10.4).

Like its big-cat predecessors, Tiger brings lots of improvements to the Mac. Things like Spotlight, the Dashboard, Automator, Safari RSS, an improved System Preferences application, tighter integration and better synchronization services with .Mac, and improved speech synthesis for accessibility. The list goes on and on. And at the system level, Apple has made a lot of refinements to the Unix layer that makes Tiger purr. For most users, those system-level changes might not mean much, but that's the way it *should* be. You should be able to boot your Mac, install and run software, and have a great time.

This new edition of the *Mac OS X Pocket Guide* is your quick reference to using Mac OS X Tiger. This book gives you a quick overview of Mac OS X Tiger, starting out by showing you what's new, before providing you with a tour of the system so you can see more of what's waiting for you. Along the way you'll learn:

- How to use the Dashboard
- How to search for and find stuff with Spotlight

- Handy keyboard shortcuts to help you be more efficient with your Mac
- How to use the Terminal to issue basic Unix commands
- And you'll also get a bunch of quick tips for setting up and configuring your Mac to really make it your own

If you're an experienced Mac user, this book may be the only one you'll need. For Mac users coming to Mac OS X from an earlier version of the Mac OS, some of the material in this book can serve as a refresher, reminding you how to do certain things you've always been able to do on the Mac. In addition, you'll learn more about the Unix side of Mac OS X and how to use its command-line interface, the Terminal application.

You'll also notice some changes from previous editions of this book. Since Mac OS X has truly evolved, I've deliberately left out details on using Classic, and on how Mac OS 9's Control Panels map over to Mac OS X's System Preferences and/or applications and utilities. As Mac OS X continues to improve and gain more features, I thought it would be best to focus this book on Mac OS X, and not so much on earlier editions of the Mac OS. If you need that information, I suggest you check out *Mac OS X: The Missing Manual, Tiger Edition*, by the world-renowned and consummate showman David Pogue.

With over 300 tips and tricks, this Pocket Guide is a handy reference for getting acquainted with, configuring, and working with Mac OS X Tiger.

Beyond This Book

One book cannot be everything to everyone, and while this book should get you started with Mac OS X Tiger, you're bound to want a deeper level of detail that a book this size just cannot provide. And when that time comes, here are some suggestions for other Mac OS X–related books you should turn to:

- *Mac OS X: The Missing Manual, Tiger Edition*, by David Pogue (Pogue Press/O'Reilly, 2005)
- *iLife '05: The Missing Manual*, by David Pogue (Pogue Press/O'Reilly, 2005)
- *iWork: The Missing Manual*, by Jim Elferdink (Pogue Press/O'Reilly, 2005)
- *iMovie HD & iDVD 5: The Missing Manual*, by David Pogue (Pogue Press/O'Reilly, 2005)
- *iPod & iTunes: The Missing Manual*, by J.D. Biersdorfer (Pogue Press/O'Reilly, 2005)
- *GarageBand 2: The Missing Manual*, by David Pogue (Pogue Press/O'Reilly, 2005)
- *AppleScript: The Missing Manual*, by Adam Goldstein (Pogue Press/O'Reilly, 2005)
- *Inside .Mac*, by Chuck Toporek (O'Reilly, 2004)
- *AppleScript: The Definitive Guide*, by Matt Neuberg (O'Reilly, 2003)

Or, if you're looking for something with more depth on the Unix side of Mac OS X, here are some titles for you to chew on:

- *Learning Unix for Mac OS X Tiger*, by Dave Taylor (O'Reilly, 2005)
- *Mac OS X Tiger for Unix Geeks*, by Brian Jepson and Ernest E. Rothman (O'Reilly, 2005)
- *Running Mac OS X Tiger*, by Jason Deraleau and James Duncan Davidson (O'Reilly, 2005)
- *Mac OS X Tiger in a Nutshell*, by Andy Lester and Chris Stone (O'Reilly, 2005)

Combined, these books run the full gamut of information to take you from Mac newbie to expert level, if you've got the time and inclination to absorb the information within. There are also countless mailing lists, run both by Apple and by others, that you can use to learn more about Mac OS X Tiger, as well as to meet other Mac users. Speaking of which, if you're new to the Mac, I'd highly recommend going to at least one or two Macintosh User Group (MUG) meetings in your area. Most major cities have at lease one MUG with meetings each month, and you'd be amazed at the wealth of information MUG members have and are willing to share.

Conventions Used in This Book

The following typographical conventions are used in this book:

Italic

> Used to indicate new terms, URLs, usernames, filenames, file extensions, Unix commands and options, program names, and directories (when viewed as a folder, the directory name is capitalized and not italicized). For example, the path in the filesystem to the Utilities folder will appear as */Applications/Utilities*.

`Constant width`

> Used to show the contents of files or the output from commands.

`Constant width bold`

> Used in examples and tables to show commands or other text that should be typed literally by the user.

`Constant width italic`

> Used in examples and tables to show text that should be replaced with user-supplied values; also used to show text that varies in menus.

Bold

> Used to indicate features, commands, and options in lists that highlight new or improved functionality .

Variable lists

The variable lists throughout this book present answers to "How do I..." questions (e.g., "How do I change the color depth of my display?"), or offer definitions of terms and concepts.

Menus/navigation

Menus and their options are referred to in the text as File → Open, Edit → Copy, etc. Arrows will also be used to signify a navigation path when using window options; for example, System Preferences → Desktop & Screen Saver → Screen Saver means you would launch System Preferences, click on the icon for the Desktop & Screen Saver preferences panel, and select the tabbed button for the Screen Saver pane within that panel.

Pathnames

Pathnames are used to show the location of a file or application in the filesystem. Directories (equivalent to folders for Mac and Windows users) are separated by forward slashes. For example, if you see something like "launch the Terminal application (*/Applications/ Utilities*)" in the text, that means the Terminal application can be found in the Utilities subfolder of the Applications folder.

~

The tilde character (~) refers to the current user's Home folder. So, if you see something like *~/Library* or *~/ Pictures*, that means you should go to the Library or Pictures folder, respectively, within your own Home folder. This is a much shorter representation than showing the entire path to the folder (which would be */Macintosh HD/Users/username/Library* for the *~/Library* folder).

↵

A carriage return (↵) at the end of a line of code is used to denote an unnatural line break; that is, you should not enter these as two lines of code, but as one continuous

line. Multiple lines are used in these cases due to printing constraints.

$, #

The dollar sign ($) is used in some examples to show the
user prompt for the bash shell; the hash mark (#) is the
prompt for the root user.

TIP

Indicates a tip, suggestion, or general note.

WARNING

Indicates a warning or caution.

Menu symbols

When looking at the menus for any application, you will
see some symbols associated with keyboard shortcuts for
a particular command. For example, to open a document in Microsoft Word, you could go to the File menu
and select Open (File → Open), or you could issue the
keyboard shortcut, ⌘-O.

Figure 1 shows the symbols used in the various menus to
denote a keyboard shortcut.

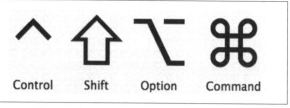

*Figure 1. These symbols are used in Mac OS X's menus for issuing
keyboard shortcuts so you can quickly work with an application
without having to use the mouse.*

Rarely will you see the Control symbol used as a menu command option; it's more often used either in association with mouse clicks to emulate a right-click on a two-button mouse or for working with the *bash* shell.

PART I

What's New in Tiger?

Long before releasing Mac OS X Tiger, Apple offered a preview to developers and also posted some information about Tiger's top features on the OS X web site (*http://www.apple.com/macosx*). But just in case you missed the big list of features, here's another rundown of what's in store for you:

- **Dashboard** puts everything you need at your fingertips, in a dash. Dashboard comes with a set of "widgets" that give you instant access to local weather reports or even the Yellow Pages. See the "Dashboard" section, later in this book, for more details.

- **Automator** lets you create "actions" that use multiple applications to do complex tasks for you.

- **Spotlight** helps you find stuff quickly and easily by indexing and cataloging content in all of the files on your system. Spotlight's search capabilities are built into the Finder, System Preferences, and many applications, including Mail and Address Book.

- **Parental Controls** lets you manage users and restrict their access to things (for example, by allowing them to view only administrator-approved web sites or controlling with whom they can chat over iChat).

- **VoiceOver** provides powerful accessibility features for persons with physical disabilities.

- **Safari** continues to improve, and with Tiger, it now supports RSS and Atom syndication protocols, automatically letting you know that a site has a news feed you can subscribe to. When you visit a web site with an RSS/Atom feed, a blue RSS icon pops up in Safari's address bar; click the RSS icon to see the site's feed.

- **QuickTime** with H.264 is a new MPEG encoding method that allows videos to be scaled up or down to run on everything from high-definition (HD) televisions to cellular phones.

- Speaking of H.264, the new version of **iChat AV** uses this encoding method to provide higher quality audio and video for your chats. And the new version of iChat also works with Jabber, and supports audio chats with up to 10 people and video chats with up to 4 people (including yourself). This makes using iChat a great way to keep in touch with friends, family, and coworkers.

- **Migration Assistant** allows you to migrate data to Tiger from another Mac or disk partition.

- **.Mac Sync** enables you to keep valuable data on Macs, portable devices, and .Mac accounts up to date.

- **Xcode 2.0** provides sweeping changes for the way programmers develop applications, allowing them to create apps more quickly and take advantage of new Apple technologies.

  Developers also get a new set of application programming interfaces (APIs), including Core Data, Core Image, Core Video, and a new .Mac SDK that allows non-Apple developers to create applications that work with the .Mac services.

NOTE

If you're a developer and you're interested in learning more about the new APIs for Tiger, you should visit the Apple Developer Connection (ADC) web site, at *http://developer.apple.com*.

- If you thought iPhoto's Smart Folders were great, just wait and see what **Smart Folders** and **Burn Folders** let you do in Tiger. You can even create special "Burn Folders" to quickly burn files to CD or DVD without first having to create a disk image.
- A totally new **Mail** application allows you to create Smart Mail Folders and manage your accounts better.
- More power to **Unix** with an improved kernel for more speed, 64-bit enhancements for Macs with G5 processors, and new utilities.
- Changes to old standby apps like Address Book, iCal, iSync, iChat, etc.
- Lots of little enhancements, including tweaks to the Finder, search capability built into System Preferences, and .Mac Sync, to name a few.

Whew! And that's just for starters! In total, Apple boasts that over 150 new features have been added to Mac OS X Tiger, and while some might not be so evident from the surface, you'll definitely find little gems along the way. Whether it's a vast speed improvement in Tiger's startup time or some seemingly minor new feature for your favorite application, Tiger has something to make all Mac users purr.

Cool New Features in Tiger

Okay, so you've already heard about some of the bigger features added to Mac OS X Tiger—Spotlight, Automator, Dashboard, VoiceOver, etc.—but Apple had plenty more up its sleeves. For example, these are some of the lesser-known features Apple has added to Tiger:

Use Tiger's built-in dictionary
    This allows you to look up any word in a file you have open. All you need to do is move your mouse over a

word, and then hold down Control-⌘-D. A dictionary pop-up window appears (Figure 2), showing you a full dictionary-style definition for the word beneath the mouse pointer. This is particularly handy when someone sends you a file that's full of big words you don't know. Try moving your mouse around and watch as the pop-up window changes to the definition of a new word.

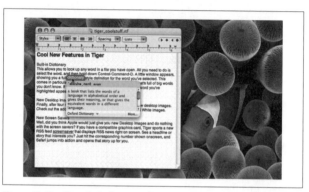

Figure 2. Use Tiger's built-in Oxford Dictionary to quickly see phonetic spellings and definitions for words you don't know. The pop up also features a Thesaurus.

Flashy new Desktop images

Finally, after four versions of Mac OS X, we get to see some new Desktop images. Check out the additions to the Nature set (see the clown fish in Figure 2?) or the new Black and White images.

Way cool screensavers

Well, did you think Apple would just give you new Desktop images and do nothing with the screensavers? If you have a Quartz-compatible graphics card, Tiger sports a new screensaver that displays RSS news right onscreen (see Figure 3). See a headline or story that interests you?

Just hit the corresponding number and Safari jumps into action and opens that story for you.

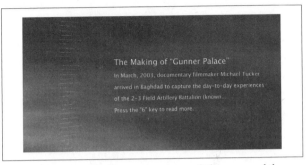

The Making of "Gunner Palace"

In March, 2003, documentary filmmaker Michael Tucker
arrived in Baghdad to capture the day-to-day experiences
of the 2-3 Field Artillery Battalion (known...
Press the "6" key to read more.

Figure 3. Tiger's new RSS screensaver not only lets you read the news from your favorite site, but also lets you quickly jump to news stories in Safari by pressing a number key.

Two new folder types

That's right, just when you thought it was safe to create an ordinary folder, it's time to think again, because Tiger introduces two new folder types: Smart Folders and Burn Folders. Yes, I know Smart Folders have been available in iPhoto and other applications, but this is the first time you can use them anywhere! For more information on these folders, see the section "Creating New Folders" in Part III.

Search with Control

Say your friend sends you an email asking what the annual rainfall in Portland, Oregon, is; how are you going to find that out? Well, in Tiger, you can select the text in the email ("annual rainfall in Portland, Oregon"), and then Control-click the text you've selected. In the contextual menu that appears (see Figure 4), you'll see two new items at the top: Search in Spotlight, and Search in Google. The Spotlight option searches for related items on your computer, while the Google option searches the entire Internet.

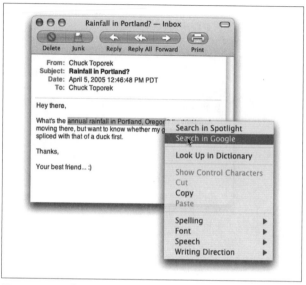

Figure 4. Just select some text and Control-click it to either search with Spotlight or search with Google.

.Mac Sync

> If you've got more than one Mac (or if you use a Mac at work and have one at home) and you have a .Mac account (*http://www.mac.com*), Tiger's .Mac preferences let you synchronize data from your Address Book, iCal, Safari's Bookmarks, your Keychains, and even your Mail (including folders, preferences, mailboxes...everything) from one computer to the other in a flash.

Shared contacts

> Beyond syncing your Address Book contacts between your work and home computer, wouldn't it be nice to share your contacts with your brother across town or a coworker in another state? While you *could* allow them to sync with your .Mac account, that's not the best idea,

since you'd also have to supply them with your password. Tiger's new Address Book allows you to share your contacts with other .Mac members. To set this up, just follow these steps:

1. To turn on contact sharing, open Address Book's preferences (Address Book → Preferences, or ⌘-,), and click the checkbox next to "Share your Address Book."

2. Click the + button and select a .Mac member to share your Address Book with.

3. Click the Send Invite button. This opens a new message in Mail that includes a link to your Address Book info.

4. When the other user receives your email message, all she needs to do is click the link. When she does, her Address Book opens, with a sheet (see Figure 5) that asks if she wants to subscribe to your Address Book.

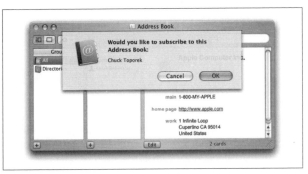

Figure 5. Just click OK to subscribe to another .Mac member's Address Book.

5. After she clicks OK, your Address Book contacts are "synced" to her Address Book.

Another option for subscribing to another .Mac member's Address Book is to select File → "Subscribe to Address Book," and type in the email address for a .Mac member (such as *eyeheartportland@mac.com*). If that user has enabled Address Book sharing for you, you'll be able to subscribe to his list of contacts.

Download your updates

There's no bigger pain than to have Software Update endlessly bouncing up and down in your Dock when some new update is released. Instead, you can now opt to have Mac OS X download those updates to your Mac in the background, letting you choose when to install them. For this, go to System Preferences → Software Update and turn on "Download important updates in the background."

Add birthdays to iCal

If you use Address Book's near-hidden feature of including a birth date in someone's record (in Address Book's menu bar, select Card → Add Field → Birthday), you can now get those birthdays to automatically show up in iCal. All you need to do is:

- Open iCal (located in your Dock or in your Applications folder).
- Open iCal's preferences (iCal → Preferences, or ⌘-,), and turn on "Show Birthdays calendar."

A new Birthdays calendar appears to the left, in iCal's list of calendars. Notice the little birthday cake icon—complete with a candle on top—to the right of the calendar name, as shown in Figure 6.

These are just some of the many new features that have been added to Mac OS X Tiger. As you work your way through this book, you'll become aware of even more, but these should give you a taste of what's to come.

Figure 6. Tiger's Address Book and iCal work together to provide you with a Birthdays calendar, so you'll never forget to send out a birthday card again.

NOTE

If you need a more in-depth look at Mac OS X Tiger, don't miss David Pogue's *Mac OS X: The Missing Manual, Tiger Edition.* David's Missing Manual series is the best in the lot if you want to learn more about your Mac, and there's no better place to start than with his book on Mac OS X (which, by the way, has been the #1 computer book in North America *three years running!*). For a complete list of the books in the Missing Manual series, and to see what else David is up to, visit *http:// www.missingmanuals.com.*

PART II

Mac OS X Survival Guide

If you're one of the many switchers who've come over to Mac OS X, or even if you've been using Mac OS X since the early public beta (back when Mac OS X was going through its infancy 10.0 and 10.1 phases), this chapter is for you. Here, you'll quickly get up to speed on how to use Mac OS X, from learning about the Finder, to learning how to create folders (including the new Smart and Burn folders), to discovering tips, tricks, and keyboard shortcuts to make your Mac life more enjoyable.

Your User Account

When you first install Mac OS X Tiger (or when you boot your new Mac for the first time), you have to create at least one user for the system. You'll be asked to assign a name, short name, and password, as well as provide address information for the user. You'll also set up some very basic preferences, such as the date and time zone, and configure basic network settings.

By default, the first user you set up on your Mac is known as an "administrative user," which means that user can pretty much do whatever he wants with the system, including setting up or removing user accounts. As an admin user, you can create accounts for other users (such as your wife and kids) on your system, manage their settings, and also delete their accounts when necessary.

After you create the admin user account, Mac OS X logs into
that account, and then you're off and running. And every
time you boot your Mac, the system automatically logs into
this account unless you add another user account or change
the settings in the Accounts preference panel (System Preferences → Accounts).

What's in Your Home Folder?

Regardless of how many users are on your system, every
user's Home folder is really a subfolder within the Users
folder. For example, if you have two users on your system
whose short names (which are assigned when you create user
accounts) are *chuck* and *bob*, their Home folders show up in
the Finder by navigating to Macintosh HD → Users →
username (in this case, either *chuck* or *bob*).

Every user on a Mac OS X system has a default set of folders,
found within her own Home folder. These folders can be
used for storing anything you desire, although some have
specific purposes, as noted here:

Desktop
   While you might think of your desktop as that thing that
   sits beneath all the windows on your Mac, it is actually a
   folder in itself. The Desktop folder contains the items
   found on your desktop, including any files, folders, or
   application aliases you've placed there.

Is Automatic Login Secure?

The short answer to that is: No. If your Mac is set up to automatically log on to your user account, all somebody needs to do is boot your machine and he has easy access to all your information. While this might not seem like such an issue if you're using your Mac at home, think again. If someone breaks into your house or apartment and steals your beloved Mac, the thief not only has your computer, but automatic login gives him free reign over all your info.

If you're security conscious and you don't want the system to automatically log in to your account (or that of another user) at startup, you can disable this setting by going to the Accounts panel, clicking Login Options, and turning off the checkbox next to "Automatically log in as".

Right above that you'll see options for how the Login Window appears at startup. You can set this so the Login Window displays a list of users or requires users to enter both their username and password. With the "List of users" option, the Login Window displays a list of users for the system, along with any graphical icon they've set for their user account. To log in, simply click on the appropriate username (the others then disappear), enter the password in the space provided, and then either hit Return or click the Log In button.

Of the two options, "List of users" is probably the least secure, because all someone needs to do is guess your password. By requiring users to enter *both* their username and password, you ensure that they actually know the short username for the user account. Just because my name is Chuck Toporek doesn't necessarily mean that's the name I use for my account (as defined in the Short Name field of the Accounts panel).

And if you're really paranoid (like me), you should enable FileVault protection for your user account, using the Security preference panel (System Preferences → Security). For more information about the Security panel and FileVault, see the "Security" section, later in Part II.

Documents

> While it isn't mandatory, the Documents folder can be used as a repository for any files or folders you create. Most applications, such as TextEdit, Microsoft Word, and the new iWork's Pages application, save files here by default.

Library

> This folder contains preference files, known in Mac OS X land as *property lists files*, or *plist* files (so-named because of their *.plist* file extension). These plist files are used by applications to store the preferences you set.

Movies

> This is a place where you can store movies you create with iMovie, DVD projects you create with iDVD, or where you can hold QuickTime movies you create or download from the Internet.

Music

> This directory is used to store music and sound files, including *.aiff*, *.mp3*, etc. This is also where your iTunes Library, and the music you purchase through the iTunes Music Store, are located.

Pictures

This directory can be used as a place to store photos and other images. iPhoto also uses the Pictures directory to store your iPhoto Library.

Public

If you enable file or web sharing (System Preferences → Sharing), this is where you place items you want to share with other users on your system. Users who access your Public folder can see and copy items from this directory.

Also located within the Public folder is the Drop Box folder. If you enable File Sharing (System Preferences → Sharing → Services → File Sharing), this is where other users can place files after connecting to your Mac.

Sites

If you enable Personal Web Sharing (System Preferences → Sharing → Services), this folder will contain the web site for your user account.

If your system has more than one user on it, you'll find a Shared folder within the Users folder. Because users are allowed to add or modify files only within their own Home folders, this is a place where you can place items to be shared with the other users.

Logging In and Fast User Switching

If you have more than one user on your system, you can enable Fast User Switching in the Accounts preference panel (System Preferences → Accounts). In the left column of the Accounts panel, click the Login Options button at the very bottom. This switches the panel's view to the right, which allows you to enable and configure the settings for how users log in to your system.

By default, Mac OS X has the "Automatically log in as" option checked, and you should see your username in the pop-up menu next to this item. If you have more than one user on your Mac, and you're not sure who will log in when, you should uncheck this option.

Sleep Mode, Logging Out, and Shutting Down

When you've reached the end of your day, you've got three options for dealing with your Mac. You can:

- Log out of your account (Shift-⌘-Q), which takes you out of your user environment, placing you at a login screen where you'll need to enter your username and password to gain access to the system again.

- Shut down the system by selecting ⌘ → Shut Down. Selecting this option logs you out of your user account and powers off your Mac.

- Put your Mac to sleep by selecting ⌘ → Sleep. If you have a PowerBook or iBook, you can just close the display (or "lid") of your laptop and your Mac automatically goes into Sleep mode.

Do you need to shut down at the end of every day? No, not really. Depending on how you've configured the Energy Saver preferences (System Preferences → Energy Saver), you can just put your Mac to sleep every night, or let it fall asleep based on the preference settings you've made, and everything should be okay.

NOTE

It's very common for Mac users to reboot (or restart) Mac OS X only when there is a critical Software Update that forces you to restart, such as a Security Update or an upgrade to a newer version of Mac OS X.

The advantage to putting your Mac into Sleep mode is that it keeps the system running so you don't have to wait for your Mac to start up again (not that it takes very long for Mac OS X to boot anyway). In Sleep mode, your Mac uses a very minimal amount of energy to keep the system running, which saves you (or your company) money in the long run. To wake your Mac up from Sleep mode, just hit the Return key on your keyboard. The hard drive spins up, and your Mac jumps back to life, ready for you to go to work.

Startup and Shutdown Keys

For most users, starting and shutting down your Mac is fairly routine: press the Power-On button to start, and go to → Shut Down to turn your Mac off at night. But there are times when you need to do more, for whatever reason. Table 1 lists some of the additional keys you can use when starting, restarting, logging out, and shutting down your system.

NOTE

Some of the keyboard shortcuts listed in Table 1 only work on newer hardware. If you are using an older Mac, these keyboard shortcuts might not work.

Table 1. Keyboard shortcuts used for starting, restarting, logging out, and shutting down

Key command	Description
C	Holding down the C key at startup boots from a CD or DVD (useful when installing or upgrading the system software).
N	Attempts to start up from a NetBoot server.
R	Resets the display for a PowerBook.
T	Holding down the T key at startup places your Mac into Target Mode as a mountable FireWire drive. After starting up, your screen will have a blue background with a floating yellow FireWire symbol. Target mode makes the hard drive(s) of your Mac appear as mounted FireWire drive(s) when connected to another system. To exit Target mode, press the Power-On button to turn off your Mac. After your Mac has shut down completely, press the Power-On button again to restart your Mac.
X	Holding down the X key at startup forces your Mac to boot into Mac OS X, even if Mac OS 9 is specified as the default startup disk.
⌘-S	Boots into *single-user mode* (something you'll only need to do when troubleshooting your system, or if you're a system administrator).
⌘-V	Boots into *verbose mode*, displaying all the startup messages onscreen. (Linux users will be familiar with this.)
Shift	Holding down the Shift key at startup invokes Safe Boot mode, turning off any unnecessary kernel extensions (*kexts*) and ignoring anything you've set in the Accounts preferences panel.
Option	Holding down the Option key at startup opens the Startup Manager, which allows you to select which OS to boot into.
Mouse button	Holding down the mouse button at startup ejects any disk (CD, DVD, or other removable media) that might still be in the drive.
Shift-Option-⌘-Q Option + 🍎 → Log Out Option-Power-On	Logs you off without first prompting you.
Option + 🍎 → Shut Down	Shuts down your system without first prompting you.

Table 1. Keyboard shortcuts used for starting, restarting, logging out, and shutting down (continued)

Key command	Description
Option + ⌘ → Restart	Restarts your machine without first prompting you.
Control-⌘-Power-On	Forces an automatic shutdown of your system; this should be used only as a last resort because it could mess up your filesystem.[a]
Control-Eject (F12)	Opens a dialog box that contains options for Restart, Sleep, and Shutdown.
Control-Option-⌘-Eject (F12)	Quits all applications and shuts the system down. If there are any application windows open with unsaved changes, you will be prompted to save the changes before the application is forced to quit.

[a] Mostly, you'll just wait at the gray Apple startup screen while a Unix command (*fsck*, short for *filesystem check*) runs in the background, cleaning up any goobers on your system.

Quick Tips for Users

Here are some helpful hints to assist you in managing your user account:

Configure my login?
System Preferences → Accounts → *username* → Login Options.

Change my login password?
System Preferences → Accounts → *username* → Password.

NOTE

When choosing a password, you should avoid using dictionary words (i.e., common, everyday words found in the dictionary) or something that could be easily guessed. To improve your security, choose an alphanumeric password. Remember, passwords are case-sensitive, so you can mix upper- and lowercase letters in your password as well.

Add another user to the system?
System Preferences → Accounts → click on the plus sign (+) below the Login Options button (requires administrator privileges).

NOTE

Unix administrators might be tempted to use the *useradd*, *userdel*, and *usermod* commands to add, remove, and modify a user, respectively, from the Terminal. The only problem is, you can't; these commands don't exist on Mac OS X.

Remove a user from the system?

System Preferences → Accounts → *username* → click on the minus sign (–) below the Login Options button (requires administrator privileges). After a user has been deleted, that user's directories (and everything within) are packaged up in a disk image (as *username.dmg*) and placed in the */Users/Deleted Users* folder. Only a user with administrator privileges can delete this disk image.

NOTE

Obviously, you can't remove your own user account when you're logged into system. If you want to remove your user account from the system, you have to log out and log back in as another user.

Give a user administrator privileges?

System Preferences → Accounts → *username* → Password → turn on the checkbox next to "Allow user to administer this computer" (requires administrator privileges).

Restrict which applications a user can use?

System Preferences → Accounts → *username* → Parental Controls (this pane isn't available if the user has administrator privileges). The Parental Controls pane gives you five options, which are discussed in the "Parental Controls" section, later in Part II.

Keep a user from changing her password?

System Preferences → Accounts → *username* → Parental Controls → turn on Finder & System.

Turn off automatic login?
> System Preferences → Accounts → *username* → Login Options → uncheck the box next to "Log in automatically as *username*."

Allow a user to log in to my Mac from a Windows system?
> System Preferences → Sharing → Services → check the box next to Windows Sharing.

Turn on Fast User Switching?
> System Preferences → Accounts → *username* → Login Options → click on the checkboxes next to "Automatically log in as..." and "Enable fast user switching."

Set a password hint?
> System Preferences → Accounts → *username* → Password → Change Password. When you click on the Change Password button, a sheet slides down from the titlebar, asking you to provide your current password; enter your password and then tab down to the Password Hint field; just enter some text in this field and hit Return to save the change.

Find out which users have admin privileges?
> System Preferences → Accounts. Users with administrator privileges have the word "Admin" beneath their name in the list of users in the left column. Unrestricted users will have the word "Standard" beneath their username, and users who have Parental Controls enabled on their account will have the word "Managed" beneath their username.

Parental Controls

New to Mac OS X Tiger is a set of Parental Controls, which you can apply to non-administrator user accounts on your Mac. Parental Controls, which are enabled via the Accounts → Parental Controls preference panel, allow you to restrict the actions of non-administrative users on your Mac. To enable one of the Parental Controls, click the checkbox and then click the Configure button to the right (or Info button, in the case of the Dictionary item) to alter the settings for managing the user. The five options you're presented with include:

Mail

Restrict which addresses this user can send email to. There's also a feature (which is turned on by default) that first sends the email to another person (presumably the parent or system administrator), who can grant permission for the email to be sent to the original address.

Finder and System

When enabled, this panel opens a sheet that allows you to determine whether the user will have Some Limits, or if they'll see the Simple Finder when they log in. You can also restrict the user's access to certain applications, prevent him from modifying the Dock, or even keep him from burning CDs or DVDs.

NOTE

Keep the Simple Finder in mind if you have a user you'd like to restrict from issuing Unix commands. You can cut off a user's access to the Terminal application by clicking the disclosure triangle next to Utilities and then turning off the checkbox next to the Terminal application.

---

iChat

This lets you specify a pre-approved list of people with whom the user is allowed to chat over iChat.

Safari

This restricts the user from going to any web site that hasn't been added to her bookmark list by an administrative user. When a user tries to go to a web site that hasn't been bookmarked and approved by an admin user, the user is prompted to enter the admin user's username and password. If authentication is successful, the user can go to and bookmark the site; otherwise, the user sees a mes-

---

sage in Safari's window informing her that she is restricted from using the site.

Dictionary

With this option enabled, the user is restricted from viewing certain words in the Dictionary application, such as profanity (think of George Carlin's "Seven Words You Can't Say on Television" routine), as well as some slang terms for various body parts.

TIP

Before you can turn on Parental Controls, the user to whom you're trying to apply restrictions must be logged out.

Using Software Update

From time to time, Apple releases patches to Mac OS X and its other applications, such as the iLife apps, and, on occasion, security patches to block holes that could put your Mac (and the data on it) at risk. To keep your system up-to-date, Apple provides a Software Update application (accessible either through the System Preferences → Software Update preference panel or via → Software Update).

NOTE

Whenever you install a new version of Mac OS X, or any Apple application for that matter, it's always wise to run Software Update to see if there's a new patch for your system.

Software Update's preference panel, shown in Figure 7, gives you the option of checking for updates Daily, Weekly, or Monthly. When you click Check Now, Software Update records the day and time that you checked for updates, and uses this information as the basis of when to check for the next update. For example, if you have Software Update set to look for updates Daily (through the "Check for updates" pop-up menu), and the last time you checked for an update was yesterday at 7:53 a.m., it'll automatically check for updates at that time every day.

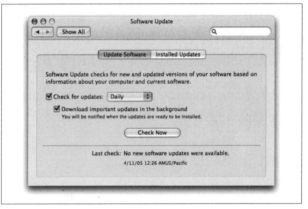

Figure 7. Use the Software Update panel to keep your system (and any Apple applications you're running) up-to-date.

You also have the option to have Software Update automatically "Download important updates in the background" by turning on its checkbox. With this option enabled, Software Update checks for updates on its regularly scheduled basis and if it finds something critical you need (like a Security Update that protects your Mac), Software Update automatically downloads that item to your system. Once the item has downloaded, a dialog box appears, giving you the option to install the update at your leisure.

Security

Mac OS X Tiger offers some powerful built-in security features that every user should take advantage of. Regardless of whether your Mac is at work or home, or if you never ever go

Saving Your Updates

If you manage more than one Mac system (for example, your Power Mac G5, your wife's iBook, and your kids' eMac), running Software Update on all the machines not only takes each person a lot of time, but also taps out your bandwidth. One solution to this problem is to download the updates from Apple's Mac OS X software page, found online at *http://www.apple.com/downloads/macosx*. You'll not only find the latest updates and software patches here, but you'll also find Combo Updates for Mac OS X, each of which are downloadable as disk images that can be burned to CD or DVD. Once you've burned those disk images, you can then take the CD or DVD to each machine and install the update by mounting the disk image and double-clicking the installer.

Mac OS X's Combo Updates come in particularly handy when you need to do a clean install on a system. For example, say that Apple releases an update to Mac OS X Tiger, putting it at Version 10.4.3, but you decide that it's time to do a clean install, reformat your hard drive, and maybe partition your hard drive (see *Running Mac OS X Tiger* [O'Reilly, 2005] for details on how to do that). When you gut your system like that, you'll need to do a fresh install of Tiger, which means you're back to Version 10.4. And while you could run Software Update and install all the updates from there, if you've burned the latest Combo Update to CD, you can just pop in that disc and double-click the installer.

online, there are some basic things you should consider setting up on your Mac to protect your user account and your precious data.

FileVault

Introduced with Mac OS X Panther (Version 10.3), FileVault allows you to encrypt and protect everything within your Home folder. FileVault uses a 128-bit data encryption scheme, which means it's very hard to crack. To enable FileVault for your user account, go to the Security preferences panel and click the Turn On FileVault button. FileVault uses your login password as the passkey to secure the data in your Home folder. While you're at it, you should also click the Set Master Password button to set a master password that allows you to unlock any FileVault account on your computer.

The one caveat to using FileVault is that if you forget your password and you haven't set the Master Password (or if you forget both passwords), there is absolutely no way to decrypt your FileVault-protected Home folder. If you can't remember either password, all of your data is lost. If you are going to use FileVault, you should write these passwords down and hide them from plain sight (or in your bank's safety deposit box, if you have one). That way, if you ever do forget your passwords, you'll at least (hopefully) remember where you wrote them down so you can retrieve your data.

Keychains

Just like the keys you carry in your pocket to unlock your house or start your car, the Mac OS X Keychain service helps you manage and keep track of all the usernames and passwords you have for everything from your user account to the information you provide to log on to your favorite web site or network file server. Keychains have been around since Mac OS 9 and have continued to improve along with Mac OS X.

Every user has a Keychain file, which is stored in your Home → Library → Keychains folder. The Keychain file is encrypted and can only be viewed with the aid of the Keychain Access program (*/Applications/Utilities*). You can use this program to add or delete items in your Keychain, create and store an encrypted note, and more. New to Keychain Access for Mac OS X Tiger is the ability to search for specific items in your Keychain. This is a great improvement because, in the past, you'd have to sift through the items in your Keychain and hope to find what you were looking for.

Keep Keychain Access in mind for those times when you've forgotten a password to something. Chances are, if you've had to authenticate yourself to a web site, the information you need is stored in your Keychain.

TIP

Because your Keychain contains all of your passwords (and maybe that encrypted note, ranting about your boss), you should consider backing up your Keychain regularly. There are many ways to do this, such as backing it up to your iDisk (if you have a .Mac account) or dragging the Home → Library → Keychains folder to an external drive.

If you're feeling a little less secure about these ideas, you might consider using Disk Utility (*/Applications/Utilities*) to create an encrypted and password-protected disk image of your Keychains folder.

Firewall Settings

If you're taking your Mac online—regardless of whether you're at home or at work—you really should enable Mac OS X's built-in firewall. Basically, a firewall protects your Mac from unwanted intrusions from people trying to pry into your Mac and steal your data while you're online. Even though Macs are more secure than most Windows PCs, you're still prone to attacks, especially if you use a broadband connection to the Internet, such as DSL or cable modem.

To enable Mac OS X's firewall:

1. Launch System Preferences by clicking on its icon in the Dock.
2. Select the Sharing preference panel.
3. Click the Firewall tab.
4. Click the Start button.

It's that easy.

Beneath the Start button you'll see a list of various ports for services for which you can allow access through your firewall. For example, if you use iChat, you should consider allowing access to your computer for iChat AV (port 19680) and iChat Bonjour (ports 5297 and 5298), if you care to use iChat over a Bonjour network.

What the Heck Is Bonjour?

Until Mac OS X Tiger came along, Bonjour was known as Rendezvous, which is just another marketing name for a thing called Zero Configuration (or Zeroconf), which Apple built into Mac OS X Jaguar. Rendezvous (and now Bonjour) is based on an open source protocol that allows computers on the same network to talk to one another and share devices such as printers and scanners. The new name will take some getting used to, so just try to drill it into your head: "Bonjour was Rendezvous, Rendezvous is Bonjour."

Tiger offers an additional set of security features, which you access by clicking the Advanced button, located in the Sharing preference's Firewall tab. These new features include:

Block UDP Traffic

> This prevents UDP communications from accessing data on your computer. UDP stands for Universal Data Protocol, which is often exploited by crackers who want to do bad things with your computer.

Enable Firewall Logging

> This turns on firewall logging and provides you with details about any attempts some punk might have made to break through your firewall. Click Open Log to view the log file (*/var/log/ipfw.log*) in the Console application.

Enable Stealth Mode
> With Stealth Mode turned on, if anyone attempts to gain access to your computer, he won't even get a response that your computer exists. Think of this as an invisibility cloak for your computer; you can go on the network/Internet, and anyone that tries to access your computer illegally from the opposite end won't even see your computer there.

Apple wouldn't have provided these options without good reason, so if you want to protect yourself—and your computer—you should consider turning on all three of these options.

Sharing Services

As shown in the previous section, the Sharing preference panel lets you configure the firewall settings for your Mac, but you can allow additional access to your Mac through the Services tab (System Preferences → Sharing → Services). By default, all of the services listed in this pane are unchecked; to enable a service, just click the checkbox. The options provided here include:

Personal File Sharing
> Allows users of other computers to access your Public folder, located within your Home folder.

Windows Sharing
> Allows selected Windows users access to shared folders on your Mac and also enables them to print to any shared printers you've configured.

Personal Web Sharing
> When enabled, allows people to view any web pages you've saved in your Sites folder.

Remote Login
> Allows you to log on to your Mac remotely, using the Secure Shell (SSH) from a Unix shell program.

FTP Access

Allows users to download and upload files to your computer using the File Transfer Protocol (FTP).

Apple Remote Desktop

Allows others to access your computer using Apple Remote Desktop (*http://www.apple.com/remotedesktop*). If someone is using ARD, he can view everything you're doing on your computer and he can also take control of your Mac.

NOTE

Most Mac users won't use ARD; however, in larger corporate environments it's fairly common for system administrators to use ARD to help users get out of a mess or to install applications and software updates.

Remote Apple Events

Allows applications on other Macs to send remote Apple Events to your computer. Apple Events are little messages a program can send via AppleScript to your computer or to any application on your computer.

NOTE

To learn more about Apple Events and AppleScript, see *AppleScript: The Missing Manual* (Pogue Press/O'Reilly, 2005) or *AppleScript: The Definitive Guide* (O'Reilly, 2003).

Printer Sharing

Allows you to share print services with other Mac computers on your network. If you need to allow sharing to a Windows PC, don't forget to enable the Windows Sharing option, mentioned earlier in this list.

Xgrid

When enabled, an Xgrid controller can add your Mac as a distributed computing node to harness your Mac's

---

processing power. Most home users won't have to worry about enabling this service, but if you're in a work environment—particularly if you're surrounded by scientists, engineers, and software developers who are also using Mac OS X Tiger—you'd be wise to leave this option turned off; otherwise you might notice your Mac slowing down when you least expect it.

These items are disabled by default, mainly because enabling them opens up a network port to your computer, allowing other computer users to gain access to your Mac. Enable these services judiciously. For example, you might want to turn on Personal File Sharing only when you need to share files with another user. Then, as soon as you've swapped files, don't forget to turn off Personal File Sharing.

Remember, the fewer network ports you have open to your Mac, the less likely you are to have some intruder gain access and wreak havoc on your system.

Other Security Features

Some other things you can do to protect your Mac against possible intruders include turning on the following options found in the Security preference panel (System Preferences → Security):

"Require password to wake this computer from sleep or screen saver"

This way you can enable the screen saver or put your Mac to sleep ($\bullet$ → Sleep) when you know you're going to be away from your Mac, even for a small amount of time. If someone tries to use your computer or wake it from sleep, she'll be prompted to give your password, and if she doesn't know it, she won't be able to gain access to your Mac.

"Disable automatic login"

Remember, by disabling automatic login, you force users to authenticate with their username and password at login.

"Require password to unlock each secure system preference"

By enabling this option, you force users to authenticate with a valid password before they can use any of the following preference panels: Security, Energy Saver, Print & Fax, Network, Sharing, Accounts, Date & Time, and Startup Disk. This keeps unwanted users from doing such malicious things as opening ports in your firewall (Sharing → Firewall), creating or deleting user accounts, or disabling your screen saver, to name a few. Anyone who tries to access these preference panels will see a locked padlock icon in the lower-left corner. In order to use that panel, you need to click the padlock and authenticate with the current user's password.

"Log out after XX minutes of inactivity"

With this option you can specify a number of minutes (in place of the *XX*) your Mac must be inactive for the system to automatically log you out of your account. By default, this option is set to 60 minutes, but you can change this to anything from 1 minute up to 960 minutes (16 hours).

"Use secure virtual memory"

This option, new for Tiger, prevents others from being able to read any virtual memory data left on your hard drive. After enabling this feature, you must restart your Mac for this to start working.

Just remember that if someone really wants to get at the data on your Mac, there's a way around every security feature (crackers are pretty smart, you know), but enabling the above options should help you safeguard your Mac against most intrusions.

Password Security

Finally, one of the last things you can do to protect your data is to use a secure password for your user account. When choosing a password, try not to use something that's a common word, typically found in any dictionary. You should try to use a password that's an alphanumeric series of characters, using a combination of numbers and upper- and lowercase letters; for example, x41Lm89z (or something along those lines).

To help you choose a secure password, Tiger offers a Password Assistant (System Preferences → Accounts → *username* → Change Password → click the key icon next to New Password), which you can use to test the strength of your existing password. If it's weak, you can use the Password Assistant to help you find a more secure one. For details on using the Password Assistant, see Part VII.

NOTE

If you're going to write down your passwords somewhere, it's always a good idea not to keep these in the same place as your computer (such as your laptop bag or in a notebook right next to your precious iMac G5). If someone gets your passwords, he has the "keys" to all your information.

Force Quitting Applications

Every now and then, it's bound to happen: you're going to be faced with what's known in Mac circles as the "spinning beach ball of death." You know, that little colored disc that spins around in circles whenever you launch an application? Well, if you're familiar with that, someday, somehow, you'll see it "hang," and just keep on spinning. When that happens, there are a variety of things that could be going on, but it usually just means that an application got stuck doing whatever it was you wanted it to. And when an application is stuck, and you're faced with the spinning beach ball of death, you're going to need to know how to force that application to quit so you can try all over again.

Fortunately, Mac OS X has something known as *protected memory*, which means that every application—including the actual system software—runs in its own protected space. When an application hangs, it typically won't affect the system or any other apps you're running. This is a good thing, and you have the engineers at Apple to thank for it.

There are a few ways to force quit an application, but the easiest way (especially if you're not a Unix geek) is to use Mac OS X's Force Quit Applications window, which you open by either selecting → Force Quit or using its keyboard shortcut, Option-⌘-Esc. Once this window opens, all you need to do is select the application that's giving you grief and then click the Force Quit button.

TIP

Since you'll most likely be *in* the application you need to force quit, try adding the Shift key to that combination (so, Shift-Option-⌘-Esc). By adding the Shift key, you automatically quit the frontmost application. Just be careful when using this, because you could inadvertently quit the wrong application.

Relaunching the Finder

If the Finder seems to hang on you (this can sometimes happen when trying to use the Finder to connect to an FTP site), you'll need to *relaunch* the Finder.

Since the mouse pointer has been replaced with the spinning beach ball of death, chances are you won't be able to click the Apple menu (), so just use the Option-⌘-Esc shortcut to open the Force Quit Applications window. Select the

---

Finder in the list and click the Relaunch button. There is a short pause as the system takes the Finder out of commission temporarily, and you'll see the Dock disappear momentarily. When the Dock pops back into place, that's your cue that the Finder has relaunched successfully and is safe to use once more.

NOTE

You cannot use Shift-Option-⌘-Esc to relaunch the Finder. Try as you might, that shortcut just won't work. Instead, you most definitely need to use Option-⌘-Esc.

Keyboard Shortcuts

On the Mac (as with Windows and Linux desktops) you have two ways of invoking commands in the GUI: by using the menus or by issuing shortcuts for the commands on the keyboard. Not every menu item has a keyboard accelerator, but for the ones that do (the more common functions), using the keyboard shortcuts can save you a lot of time.

Basic Keyboard Shortcuts

Table 2 lists the common key commands found in Mac OS X. While most of these commands function the same way across all applications, some, such as ⌘-B and ⌘-I, can vary between programs, and others might work only when the Finder is active. For example, ⌘-B in Microsoft Word turns on boldface type or makes a selection bold, but in Xcode, ⌘-B builds your application. Likewise, ⌘-I in Word italicizes a word or selection, but hitting ⌘-I after selecting a file, folder, or application on the Desktop or in the Finder opens the Show Info window for the selected item.

Ten Essential Keyboard Shortcuts

Out of Table 2's huge list of keyboard shortcuts, there are ten that you'll use most often:

- ⌘-Q to quit an application
- ⌘-O to open a file while you're in an application
- ⌘-P to print documents
- ⌘-W to close windows
- ⌘-C to copy something you've selected in a file to the Clipboard
- ⌘-P to paste something you've copied to the Clipboard to another location
- ⌘-X to cut something you've selected out of a file and move it to the Clipboard
- ⌘-A to select everything in a file or folder (or all of the items on your desktop)
- ⌘-S to save a file (something you should do often)
- ⌘-Z to undo something you shouldn't have done

You'll quickly notice patterns when you use these shortcuts. For example, you'll find that ⌘-C and ⌘-V go hand in hand, as you'll often copy something first and then quickly paste it into another file, email, Sticky Note, etc. The difference between Copy (⌘-C) and Cut (⌘-X) is that the item you've copied stays put, whereas something you cut disappears. Keep this in mind as you master the fine art of moving stuff around in and between files.

And keep ⌘-Z in your back pocket for those times when you need to undo something. For example, say you've just finished writing your master's thesis and you decide you want to change the font. You quickly hit ⌘-A to select all of the text in the document, and then accidentally hit the Delete key. Poof! Everything is gone in the blink of an eye. But take heart, not all hope is lost. Just hit that faithful ⌘-Z key and your text is right back where you want it. Now hit the ⌘-S shortcut to save the file before you try again.

Once you get the hang of using keyboard shortcuts, you'll find yourself using the menu bar less and less.

Table 2. Common keyboard shortcuts

Key command	Task
Option-⌘-Escape	Open the Force Quit window
⌘-Tab	Cycle forward through active applications
⌘-Tab, Right Arrow	
Shift-⌘-Tab	Cycle backward through active applications
⌘-Tab, Left Arrow	
⌘-Space	Search with Spotlight
⌘-'	Cycle through an application's open windows
⌘-.	Cancel operation
⌘-?	Open Mac Help
⌘-[	Go back in the Finder view to the previous item
⌘-]	Go forward in the Finder view to the previous item
⌘-Up Arrow	Go to the folder that contains a selected item
Shift-⌘-G	Go to a specific folder in the Finder
⌘-A	Select all
Option-⌘-T	Hide/reveal the Finder's toolbar
⌘-C	Copy
⌘-D	Duplicate; creates a duplicate copy of a selected item. This command adds the word "copy" to the filename before the file extension. For example, if you were to select the file *file.txt* and hit ⌘-D, a new file named *file copy.txt* (with a space in the filename) is created in the same directory as *file.txt*).
⌘-L	Create an alias of a file
Option-⌘-D	Turn Dock hiding on/off
⌘-Delete	Move item to Trash
Shift-⌘-Delete	Empty Trash
⌘-E	Eject the selected disk image, CD, etc.
F12	Eject a CD, DVD, or networked drive
⌘-F	Find
⌘-H	Hide application
⌘-I	Get Info

Table 2. Common keyboard shortcuts (continued)

Key command	Task
⌘-J	Show View options in the Finder
⌘-K	Connect to Server
Shift-⌘-K	Connect to a specific network
⌘-M	Minimize window
Option-⌘-M	Minimize all open windows for an application
⌘-N	Open a new Finder window (this is a change from earlier versions of the Mac OS, where ⌘-N was used to create new folders)
Shift-⌘-N	Create new folder
Option-⌘-N	Create new Smart Folder
⌘-O	Open file or folder; can also be used to launch applications
⌘-P	Print file
⌘-Q	Quit application
⌘-R	Show original
⌘-T	Add an item to the Finder's Sidebar
⌘-V	Paste
⌘-W	Close window
Option-⌘-W	Close all open windows for an application
⌘-X	Cut
⌘-Z	Undo
Shift-⌘-Z	Redo (not available in all applications)
Shift-⌘-A	Go to the Applications folder in the Finder
Shift-⌘-U	Go to the Utilities folder in the Finder
Shift-⌘-C	Go to Computer View in the Finder
Shift-⌘-H	Go to Home View in the Finder
Shift-⌘-I	Go to iDisk View in the Finder (requires a .Mac account)
Shift-⌘-3	Take a screenshot of the entire display
Shift-⌘-4	Make and capture a rectangular selection of the display

PART III

Mac OS X Basics

This part of the book introduces you to the key features of Mac OS X's interface. Here we'll cover:

- The menu bar
- The Dock
- Window controls
- The Finder
- Creating new folders
- The Services menu
- Exposé
- Dashboard
- Spotlight
- Get Info and file permissions

The Menu Bar

Regardless of which application you're using, Mac OS X's menu bar is always located across the top of the screen, yet for Tiger, it takes on a new look and feel. Sure, at the outset it looks the same, but if you take a bit of a closer look, you'll notice a couple big differences.

There are some standard items you'll always find in the menu bar, but as you switch from application to application, you'll notice that the menu names and some of their options change according to which application is active. Figure 8 shows the menu bar as it appears when the Finder is active.

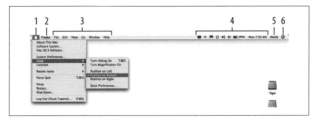

Figure 8. Mac OS X Tiger's menu bar (with the Finder active)

As Figure 8 shows, the following menus and items can be found in the menu bar. Each is covered later in Part III.

1. The Apple menu
2. The Application menu
3. A default set of application menus
4. Menu extras
5. The Accounts menu
6. Spotlight's search icon

The Apple Menu

The Apple menu, which is displayed as an apple symbol () in the menu bar, is completely different than in earlier versions of the Mac OS; you can no longer use it to store aliases for files, folders, or applications. Following is a list of what you'll find in Mac OS X's Apple menu.

About This Mac
  This option pops open a window that supplies you with information about your Mac. Aside from telling you that you're running Mac OS X on your computer, the window shows you which version of Mac OS X is installed,

how much memory you have, and the speed and type of your processor. Clicking on the More Info button launches the System Profiler (*/Applications/Utilities*), which tells you about your computer in greater detail.

Clicking on the version number in the About This Mac window reveals the build number of Mac OS X; click it again and you'll see the hardware serial number for your computer. These small details are important to have handy when contacting Apple Customer Service and when reporting a probable bug.

NOTE

In earlier versions of the Mac OS, the About box changed depending on which application was active. For information about the application, you now have to go to the Application menu (located to the right of the Apple menu) and select the About option.

Software Update

This launches the Software Update preferences panel and checks for updates for Mac OS X and other Apple software installed on your system.

Mac OS X Software

This option takes you to Apple's Mac OS X page (*http://www.apple.com/macosx*) in your default web browser.

System Preferences

This launches the System Preferences application, which replaces most of the control panels from earlier versions of the Mac OS. provides a quick run-through of the various System Preferences panels.

Dock

This menu offers a quick way to change settings for the Dock (described later in Part III).

Location

This is similar to the Location Manager Control Panel from earlier versions of the Mac OS: it allows you to change locations quickly for connecting to a network and/or the Internet.

Recent Items

This menu option combines the Recent Applications and Recent Documents options from Mac OS 9's Apple menu into one convenient menu. The Clear Menu option allows you to reset the recent items from the menu.

Force Quit

Thanks to Mac OS X's protected memory, you don't have to restart the entire system if an application crashes or freezes. Instead, you can use this menu option (or Option-⌘-Esc) to open a window that lists the applications running on your system. To force quit an application, simply click on the application name, then click Force Quit.

NOTE

Unlike applications, you cannot force quit the Finder by Control-clicking its Dock icon. Instead, you need to re-launch the Finder. When you select the Finder, the Force Quit button changes to Relaunch; click that button to re-start the Finder.

Sleep

Selecting this option puts your Mac immediately into sleep mode. This is different than the settings you dictate in System Preferences → Energy Saver for auto-sleep functionality. To "wake" your computer from sleep mode, simply press any key.

Restart

This restarts your Mac. If any applications are running, the system quits them prior to shutting down. If an application has a window with unsaved changes, you are prompted to save changes before the application quits.

Shutdown

This shuts down your Mac. You can also shut down your Mac by pressing the Power-On button, which opens a dialog box with the options for restarting, shutting down, or putting your Mac to sleep.

Log Out

This option logs you out of your system and takes you back to your login screen. The keyboard shortcut to log out is Shift-⌘-Q.

The Application Menu

Immediately to the right of the Apple menu in the menu bar is the Application menu, shown in Figure 9. While the Apple menu contains commands relevant to the whole system, the Application menu, which is rendered in boldface with the name of the active application, contains commands relevant to the active application (but not to any of its windows or documents).

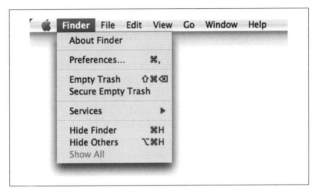

Figure 9. The Finder's Application menu

The following are some of the typical Application menu commands:

About Application Name
   Displays a small window that typically features the application's name, icon, version number, authors, copyright information, web links, and whatever else the developers felt appropriate.

Preferences...
   Calls up the application's preferences window. The standard keyboard shortcut to open an application's preferences window is ⌘-, (Command-comma).

Services
   Brings up the Services submenu, covered later in "The Services Menu."

Hide Application Name

Makes the application and all its windows (including minimized windows on the Dock) invisible and brings the next active application to the foreground. Clicking the application's Dock icon (or bringing forth any of its individual windows through its Dock menu) reveals the application once again. The standard keyboard shortcut for hiding an application is ⌘-H.

Hide Others

Hides all running Aqua applications except the current one. The standard keyboard shortcut to hide other applications is Option-⌘-H.

Show All

Reveals all hidden applications.

Quit Application Name

Quits the application. The standard keyboard shortcut to quit an application is ⌘-Q.

Standard Application Menus

In addition to the Application menu, each application (including the Finder) has at least four additional menus in the menu bar:

File

This menu contains commands for opening, creating, and saving files.

Edit

This menu contains commands for working with files, including Copy, Cut, Paste, and the all-important Undo.

Window

This menu not only keeps track of the windows an application has open, but has options for minimizing and hiding windows as well.

Help

This menu varies greatly among applications. Some applications offer just a single command, Application Help (⌘-?), which either displays the application's documentation in the Apple Help Center or performs an action of the application's own choosing.

Menu Extras

Mac OS X programs and services can place menu extras on the right side of the menu bar. Like the Apple menu, these little symbols remain constant regardless of which application you're using.

The menu extras' functions are typically reflected in their appearance and they often carry menus loaded with commands, similar to other menus. Figure 10 shows the Bluetooth menu extra.

Figure 10. The Bluetooth menu extra

The Bluetooth menu extra can be added to the menu bar from the Bluetooth preference panel (System Preferences → Bluetooth → Settings → select the checkbox next to "Show Bluetooth status in menu bar"). The Bluetooth menu extra mimics many of the functions of the Bluetooth preference panel, shows you which Bluetooth devices are within range, and offers a quick way to launch the Bluetooth File Exchange utility (*/Applications/Utilities*).

You can move a menu extra to a different location in the menu bar by Command-clicking the icon and dragging it left or right. As you move it around, the other menu extras will move out of the way to make room for it. When you let go of the mouse button, the menu extra will take its new place in the menu bar. To remove a menu extra from the menu bar, Command-click on the icon, drag it off the menu bar, and let go of the mouse button.

NOTE

For reference, executables for most of the standard menu extras can be found in */System/Library/CoreServices/Menu Extras* as folders with *.menu* extensions.

Since Mac OS X's various applications and preference panes are covered throughout this book, the ones that offer menu extras are called out in their respective descriptions.

The Accounts Menu

One of the many new features added to Mac OS X Panther was something called Fast User Switching. This lets you have multiple users logged into the system at the same time.

If your Mac has more than one user account (set up via System Preferences → Accounts), you can turn on Fast User Switching, as well as specify which user the system automatically logs in when it starts up. When you enable Fast User Switching, the Accounts menu appears at the far-right corner of the menu bar. This menu, shown in Figure 11, lists the user accounts on your Mac.

To switch to another user account, simply click on the bold-faced name of the user currently logged in and select another user account name from the Accounts menu. A login win-

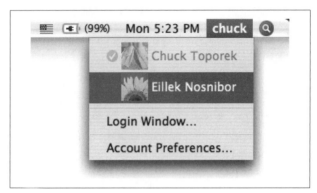

Figure 11. The Accounts menu

dow appears that prompts you for the selected user's password. If your Mac supports Quartz Extreme (and has enough RAM), your display then rotates with a 3D cube effect to the other user's desktop.

NOTE

You are required to enter a password each time you switch user accounts from the Accounts menu.

The Application Switcher

One quick way to switch between running applications—without ever moving your hands from the keyboard—is to hold down the Command key (⌘) and then press the Tab key. This pops open the Application Switcher (shown in Figure 12), which displays the icons for all the applications you have running. You'll notice, too, that there's a little white box surrounding an application icon.

The first time you press the ⌘-Tab shortcut, that box surrounds the application you were previously using. If you continue pressing the Tab key while still holding down the ⌘

Figure 12. Here you can see that the Application Switcher pops up on top of all other running applications. Continue holding down the Command key and press the Tab key to select an application; let go of the keys to bring that app to the front.

key, the white box moves right, to the next application in line. And when you get to the end of the line, the box jumps to the first icon in the Application Switcher window and continues cycling through the icons until you stop pressing the Tab key. When you let go of the ⌘-Tab keys, the application whose icon was surrounded by the white box is brought to the front so you can work with that app.

TIP

The Application Switcher is particularly helpful for times when you need to copy and paste information from one application into another. Just hit ⌘-Tab and quickly let go of the keys to switch applications in an instant. To switch back, hit ⌘-Tab again.

You can also add the Shift key to this combination (Shift-⌘-Tab) to make the little white box in the Application Switcher move backward (left) through the application icons. Following are a couple more tricks.

- Use the ⌘-Tab shortcut to open the Application Switcher, then move the mouse pointer over the application icons. As the mouse moves over each icon, the white box jumps to that icon. If you click on the icon, that app comes to the front and the Application Switcher disappears.

- With the Application Switcher open, press the Tab key to highlight an application. Continue holding the ⌘ key down and then press either **Q** to quit the application, **H** to hide the application, or **W** to close the topmost window for the application. Of course, you realize—since you're holding the ⌘ key down anyway—this is just like having that application in the foreground and pressing ⌘-Q for quit, ⌘-W to close a window, or ⌘-H to hide the application.

NOTE

Now don't get too far ahead of yourself by thinking you can issue any keyboard shortcut while you're in the Application Switcher. These (Q, W, and N) are the only three application-related keyboard shortcuts that work within the Application Switcher. For example, you can't press **N** (⌘-N) and expect a new Safari window to pop open, or **O** (⌘-O) to open a Word document, or **P** (⌘-P) to print what's in an application's window while you're in the Application Switcher. To use these commands, or do any other application-specific tasks, you'll first need to bring the respective application to the front.

Window Controls

Windows in Mac OS X have an entirely different set of controls than those from earlier versions of the Mac OS. These new window features are highlighted in Figure 13.

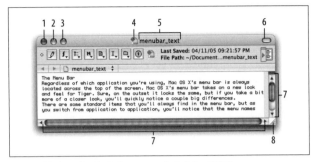

Figure 13. Standard window controls in Mac OS X

The following list identifies the controls.

1. Close window button (red)
2. Minimize window button (yellow)
3. Zoom/maximize window button (green)
4. Proxy icon
5. Filename
6. Toolbar button (not available on all windows)
7. Scrollbars and scroll arrows
8. Resize window control

The top part of the window is known as the *titlebar*. The titlebar is home to the three colored window-control buttons for closing (red), minimizing (yellow), and zooming (green) the window. When you move your mouse over the buttons, you'll notice that they take on a different appearance, becoming an ✕, a minus sign (–), or a plus sign (+). These are visual cues indicating the function that button performs.

With some applications, such as TextEdit or Microsoft Word, you'll notice that the red close window button has a dark-colored dot in its center. This little dot means the document you're working on has unsaved changes. If you save the document by selecting File → Save (⌘-S), the dot disappears.

Window Tips

The following are tips for working with windows:

Open a new window?
    File → Open (⌘-O).

Close a window?
    File → Close (⌘-W).

Close all open windows for an application?
    Option-click on the red close window button.

NOTE

If there are changes that need to be saved in any of the windows being closed, you are prompted to save the changes. Either hit Return to save the changes, or ⌘-D to invoke the Don't Save button. In some applications, a quick way to tell whether a window has unsaved changes is to look at the red close window button; if there is a dark red circle in its center, the document needs to be saved.

Minimize a window?
    Click on the yellow minimize button.

    Window → Minimize Window (⌘-M).

    Double-click on the window's titlebar.

Minimize all open windows for a single application?
    Option-⌘-M.

NOTE

With some applications, Option-⌘-M might function differently. For example, issuing Option-⌘-M in Microsoft Word (Office Versions X and 2004) opens the Paragraph format window (Format → Paragraph). Other applications that won't minimize all of the windows with this shortcut include the iChat AV, QuickTime Player, Terminal, and TextEdit. To be safe, you should save changes to the file before trying to minimize all the application's windows with Option-⌘-M.

Quickly create an alias of an open file, or move it, depending on the app (e.g., Word)?

Click and drag the file's proxy icon to a new location (i.e., the Desktop, Dock, Finder, etc.). The file must first be saved and named before an alias can be created.

TIP

Dragging a folder's proxy icon from a Finder window's titlebar moves that folder to the new location instead of creating an alias. If you want to create an alias for a folder, you should select the folder in the Finder, hold down the Option-⌘ keys, and then drag the folder to where you'd like the alias to be. As a visual cue to let you know you're creating an alias, the mouse pointer changes to a curved arrow.

Find out where a file exists in the filesystem?

Command-click on the proxy icon. This pops open a context menu showing you where the file exists. If you select another item (such as a hard drive or a folder) from the proxy icon's context menu, a Finder window opens, taking you to that location.

Hide the windows for other active applications?

Option-⌘-click on the Dock icon for the application you're using; all open windows for the other applications instantly disappear. To bring another application's windows to the front, click on that application's Dock icon; to unhide all the other windows, select Show All from the application menu of the application you're currently using (for example, select Finder → Show All).

Quickly switch from one application window to another?

Use the ⌘-` keyboard shortcut (that's a backtick, not an apostrophe). For example, if you have two Word documents open and you want to switch to the other document window after copying something, just hit ⌘-` and the other Word document window comes to the front.

The Dock

One way to think about the Dock is as part Finder, part Apple menu, and part Launcher from earlier versions of the Mac OS. The Dock, shown in Figure 14, holds application aliases, making it easy for you to launch a program quickly with a single mouse click. To launch an application in the Dock, simply click on its icon. While the application is starting its icon bounces in the Dock; after it starts, a black triangle appears below the icon to indicate that the application is running.

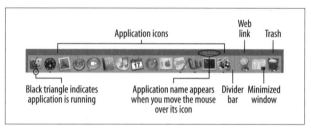

Figure 14. The Dock and its features

By default, the Dock includes icons for the Finder, Dashboard, Safari, Mail, iChat AV, Address Book, iTunes, iCal, QuickTime Player, System Preferences, and the Trash. If you need to use an application that isn't in the Dock, you'll need to open a Finder window, by clicking on its icon at the far left of the Dock (the blue smiley-face icon), and then go to the Applications folder. If you're already in the Finder, you can quickly get to the Applications folder by using its keyboard shortcut, Shift-⌘-A. Double-click the application's icon to launch the program.

To the left of the Trash icon you'll see another icon that looks like an @ symbol attached to a spring (sort of like a bobblehead). This is a quick link icon to Apple's Mac OS X web site; clicking this icon launches Safari (or whatever browser you've set as the default) and takes you to the web site. If you select and drag a URL from Safari to this area of the Dock, another springy @ icon appears with a quick link to that web site.

To add an application icon to the Dock, simply drag its icon from the Finder to the left side of the Dock's divider bar (see Figure 14) and let go. To remove an application, click on the icon and hold the mouse button down, then drag the icon away from the Dock; the icon disappears in a puff of smoke.

Dock Menus

Every active application icon has a *Dock menu*, which you can call up by either Control-clicking the icon or clicking on the icon and holding the mouse button down. An application's Dock menu is attached to its icon, as shown in Figure 15.

Dock menus contain, as commands, the titles of all the windows an application has open, each of which is marked with a little "window" symbol. Select one to bring it forth along with its parent application. The top window will have a checkmark next to it; there is no distinction for minimized windows.

Figure 15. A typical Dock menu; this one for Microsoft Word includes a list of open document windows

---

NOTE

Classic applications have only a basic Dock menu without the window list. A Classic application's Dock menu gives you only the options of Show in Finder and Quit (or Force Quit).

Every application's Dock menu typically contains at least a couple other commands, including:

Quit

Quits the application, even if it's not in the foreground. The application reacts as if you had selected Quit from its application menu or used the keyboard shortcut ⌘-Q to quit the application.

If you hold down the Option key while looking at an application's Dock menu, Quit changes to Force Quit; selecting this option kills that application instantly.

The Finder's icon lacks a Quit or Force Quit option. (In fact, all it has is a list of open Finder windows and a Hide option to hide all open Finder windows.) If you need to restart the Finder for some odd reason, do so by selecting ⌘ → Force Quit (Option-⌘-Escape). Then, select the Finder and click on the Relaunch button, as described earlier in Part III in the section "The Apple Menu."

Show In Finder

Opens a Finder window showing the location of the application on your system.

Keep In Dock

This option appears only for icons whose applications aren't permanently placed in the Dock. Normally, the icon of an undocked application vanishes once you quit the application. If you select this option, the application's icon gets a permanent home in the Dock.

Using and Configuring the Dock

Here are some helpful hints and tips for using and configuring your Dock:

Quickly resize the Dock without launching its System Preferences panel?

Place the mouse over the divider bar in the Dock; the pointer changes from an arrow to a horizontal bar with arrows pointing up and down. Click on the divider bar and move the mouse up or down to make the Dock larger or smaller, respectively.

Change the Dock's preferences?

⌘ → Dock → Dock Preferences.

System Preferences → Dock.

Control-click on the Dock's divider bar and select Dock Preferences from the context menu.

Add a program to the Dock?

Drag and drop an application's icon from a Finder window into the Dock.

After launching an application that isn't normally in the Dock, Control-click on that application's icon and select "Keep in Dock" from the pop-up menu.

Remove a program from the Dock?

Drag the application icon from the Dock and drop it anywhere.

Change the Dock's location from the bottom of the screen to the left or right side?

System Preferences → Dock → Position on screen.

 → Dock → Position on (Left, Bottom, or Right).

Control-click on the Dock's divider → Position on screen → (Left, Bottom, or Right).

Control the magnification of icons in the Dock?

System Preferences → Dock → Magnification.

 → Dock → Turn Magnification (On/Off).

Control-click the Dock's divider and select Turn Magnification (On/Off).

Make it so the Dock hides when I'm not using it?

Option-⌘-D.

System Preferences → Dock → Automatically hide and show the Dock.

 → Dock → Turn Hiding (On/Off).

Control-click the Dock's divider and select Turn Hiding (On/Off).

Stop application icons from bouncing when a program is launched?

System Preferences → Dock → uncheck the checkbox next to "Animate opening applications." Instead of the application's icon bouncing, the little black triangle

---

beneath the application icon pulses as the program launches.

Dock Tricks

The following key-mouse commands can be used when clicking on an icon in the Dock:

Command-click
> If you ⌘-click an application icon in the Dock (or just click and hold down the mouse button), the Finder will open, taking you to that application's folder.

Shift-⌘-click
> Opens a Finder window to the application's location in the filesystem. This is similar to Control-clicking a Dock icon and selecting Show In Finder from its context menu.

Control-click
> If you Control-click a running application in the Dock (or click and hold down the mouse button), a pop-up menu opens, listing the windows that the application has open, as well as options to show the application in the Finder and to Quit the application.

> If you press the Option key while Control-clicking an icon in the Dock, the Quit option toggles to Force Quit. This won't work for Classic applications (i.e., it works only for native Mac OS X applications).

Option-click
> Option-clicking has the same effect as Control-clicking, with one exception: Quit has been replaced by Force Quit in the pop-up menu.

Option-⌘-click
> Hides the windows of all other open applications and switches (if necessary) to the clicked application; similar to selecting Hide Others from the application menu.

Command-Tab

⌘-Tab opens the Application Switcher, which allows you to quickly cycle through and switch between running applications. See the section "The Application Switcher" earlier in Part III for more information.

Shift-⌘-Tab

Shift-⌘-Tab opens the Application Switcher, but works in reverse by highlighting the application icon to the left; it moves backward through running applications. See the section "The Application Switcher" earlier in Part III for more information.

NOTE

If you choose Empty Trash from the Dock by clicking on the icon and holding down the mouse button, the Trash icon's pop-up menu empties locked files as well.

Trash

Regardless of how vast and expansive you think your hard drive is, eventually you're going to run out of space. When you do, the way you get rid of any unnecessary files is by moving them to the Trash. To move a file or folder to the Trash, you can either select the item in the Finder and drag it to the Trash icon in the Dock (see Figure 14) or quickly move it to the Trash by holding down the ⌘ key and hitting the Delete key (⌘-Delete). To see what's in your Trash, just click on the Trash icon in your Dock and a Finder window pops open, revealing what's inside.

NOTE

If you happen to move the wrong file to the Trash and catch it right away, you can use Mac OS X's Undo shortcut (⌘-Z) to move the file back to where it belongs. Remember, though, you'll need to do this right away, because if you do anything else in between, the Undo applies to your last action.

To empty the Trash you can either go to the Finder's application menu and select Empty Trash (Finder → Empty Trash), or you can use Shift-⌘-Delete from within the Finder. If you've used the Finder's application menu, you've probably noticed that there's another item there, Secure Empty Trash. If you select this item, any of the files currently residing in your Trash are permanently removed from your system. But what makes this secure? Well, it doesn't just delete the file once like plain old Empty Trash does: Secure Empty Trash deletes the file and rewrites over the space where the file once was, making it nearly impossible for that file to ever be recovered.

Yes, this means that even when you've selected Empty Trash, there is a chance someone can recover that trashed file for you. It's not easy, but it can be done. With Secure Empty Trash, however, the chances of recovering that file are nil, so make sure you really want to trash that file before selecting Secure Empty Trash.

To see how to add a keyboard shortcut for Secure Empty Trash, see the "Customizing the System" section in Part VII.

Now if you go to the Finder's application menu, you'll see that the keyboard shortcut you've added for Secure Empty Trash shows up in the menu. Before using this shortcut, just make sure the files in your Trash are files you'll never, ever need again.

The Finder

Mac OS X's Finder is the main program you'll use for locating files and folders on your Mac. The Finder displays the contents of drives and folders, is used for mounting networked drives, and includes Mac OS X Tiger's powerful new search function, known as Spotlight.

The Finder's application menu (the bold Finder menu, located just to the right of the Apple menu) has options for changing the Finder's preferences (Finder → Preferences) and for emptying the Trash (Finder → Empty Trash, or Shift-⌘-Delete). The Secure Empty Trash option, added for Mac OS X Panther (Version 10.3), overwrites trashed files so they can never (ever) be recovered.

The Finder serves as a graphical file manager by offering three ways (or Views) to look at the files, folders, applications, and other filesystems (or volumes) mounted on your system. Its unique features are highlighted in Figure 16.

Mac OS X's Finder has three distinct features:

Toolbar
> Located across the top of the Finder window, the toolbar offers buttons that let you go back or forward to a previous folder or view; buttons for changing the three views (Icon, List, or Column); a button for the Action menu; and a search field for quickly finding files and folders on your Mac.

Sidebar
> Located on the left edge of the Finder window, the Sidebar offers a split view for accessing drives and other items on your Mac.
>
> The top portion of the Sidebar has icons for any kind of disk connected to your Mac. This includes hard drives and partitions, FireWire and USB drives, CDs and DVDs,

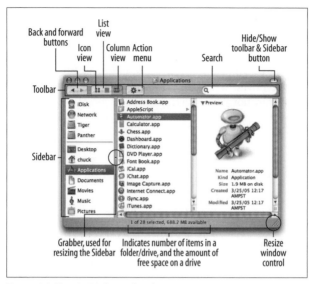

Figure 16. Tiger's Finder and its features

iDisks, disk images, and networked drives such as FTP sites or Samba shares.

The bottom portion of the Sidebar includes clickable icons for getting at your Favorites, Desktop, and Home folder, as well as items found in the Applications, Documents, Movies, Music, and Pictures folders.

The View

This area of the Finder is the big section to the right of the Sidebar. The View displays the contents of the drives and folders of your system. The default view is Icon View, which displays the files and folders as named icons; however, you can change the view to either List or Column View by clicking on the appropriate button in the toolbar.

More later on the Finder's Toolbar and Sidebar and on how to search with the Finder; for now, let's look at the three views available in the Finder.

Finder Views

As previously mentioned, the Finder has three different views for you to choose from. Each view has its own advantages. As you become more and more comfortable working with Mac OS X, you'll most likely find one you feel suits you best.

TIP

You can quickly change the Finder's viewpoint by using ⌘-1 for Icon View, ⌘-2 for List View, or ⌘-3 for Column View.

Icon View

The Icon View shows the contents of a directory as either a file, folder, or application icon, as shown in Figure 17. Double-clicking on an icon does one of three things:

- Launches an application
- Opens a file
- Displays the contents of a double-clicked folder in the Finder window

Table 3 presents a list of keyboard shortcuts for use with the Finder's Icon View.

Figure 17. The Finder, in Icon View

Table 3. Icon View's keyboard shortcuts

Key command	Description
Up, Down, Left, and Right Arrow	Move through the icons in the View based on the key pressed.
Shift-Arrow	When one icon is selected and the Shift-Arrow (Up, Down, Left, or Right) keys are pressed, the icon in that direction will be selected as well.

List View

With List View, a directory's contents are displayed in a list, as shown in Figure 18. To display the contents of a folder, you can click on the disclosure triangle (the black triangle to the left of the folder, shown in the figure).

Another way to navigate through the icons and folders in the Finder's List View is by using the keyboard shortcuts listed in Table 4.

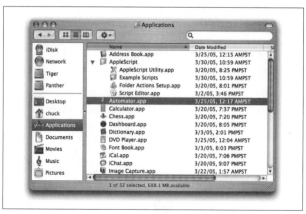

Figure 18. The Finder, in List View

Table 4. List View's keyboard shortcuts

Key command	Description
Down Arrow	Move down through the list of items.
Up Arrow	Move up through the list of items.
Right Arrow	Open a folder's disclosure triangle to reveal the folder's contents.
Left Arrow	Close a folder's disclosure triangle to hide the folder's contents.
Option–Right Arrow	Open a folder and any of its subfolders.
Option–Left Arrow	Close a folder and any of its subfolders.

To open all the folders in the View, select all the View's contents (⌘-A) and use Option–Right Arrow (likewise, use Option–Left Arrow to close them again). To open all the folders in the View, including subfolders, add the Shift key (Shift-Option–Right Arrow to open, Shift-Option–Left Arrow to close).

Column View

Column View, shown in Figure 19, displays a directory's contents in column form. This is similar to List View, except that when you click on an item, a new pane opens to the right and either exposes the contents of a folder or displays information (known as metadata) about a file, including its name, type, and file size.

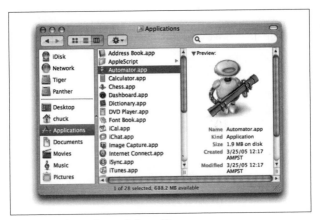

Figure 19. The Finder, in Column View

Table 5 lists the keyboard shortcuts for use with the Finder's Column View.

Table 5. Column View's keyboard shortcuts

Key command	Description
Up, Down, Left, Right Arrow	Move through the columns in the View according to the direction indicated on the key pressed.

The Finder's Sidebar

As mentioned earlier, Finder has a Sidebar (shown in Figure 16). The Sidebar has two panes located on the left side of the Finder window. The top-left pane displays whatever volumes are mounted on your Mac, including your hard drive (and any of its partitions), FireWire and USB drives, disk images, your iDisk (if you have a .Mac account), and any network volumes you might be connected to, such as an AFP, NFS, or SMB drive.

The bottom-left pane of the Sidebar includes icons to take you quickly to other folders in your Home folder, including:

- Desktop
- Your Home folder
- Applications
- Documents
- Movies
- Music
- Pictures

Volumes automatically appear in the upper portion of the Sidebar as they are mounted. To create a shortcut to a file, folder, or application, drag the item's icon to the lower portion of the Sidebar and drop it wherever you'd like. When you need to open that item (or launch the application), all you need to do is click once on the icon, just as if it were in your Dock.

To remove an item from the Sidebar, simply drag the icon away from the Finder window and let go of the mouse button; the icon disappears with a poof.

The Finder's Toolbar

Along the top of the Finder window is a toolbar (shown in Figure 16), which offers a quick way to switch between View modes and search for files on your Mac.

You can add a file, folder, or application to the Finder's toolbar by dragging and dropping its icon to the toolbar. Applications you add to the toolbar launch with a single click, just as they do in the Dock; folders open in a new Finder window.

Hiding the toolbar

Located at the upper-right corner of the Finder window is an elliptical button that can be used to hide the Finder's toolbar, as shown in Figure 20.

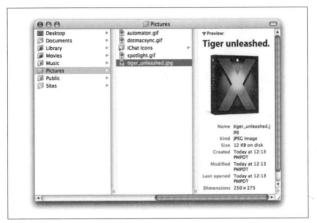

Figure 20. The Finder window with the toolbar and Sidebar hidden

In Tiger, when you click on the Hide/Show toolbar button, the Finder's toolbar behaves differently than in earlier versions of Mac OS X. If you click this button, the paned view in the Sidebar goes away and the Finder takes on a remarkable likeness to the Finders that predate Mac OS X. Click the button again and the Finder reverts to its former self. If you are in Icon or List View with the toolbar hidden, the Finder window performs just like Mac OS 9's Finder windows. Double-clicking on a folder icon opens a new window for that folder, displaying its contents. Column View functions similarly, as shown earlier in Figure 20.

Customizing the toolbar

In addition to adding shortcuts to files, folders, and applications in the toolbar, you can also customize it in other ways.

For example, if you don't like the current arrangement of buttons in the toolbar, you can ⌘-click on a button and drag it left or right. If you drag a button off the toolbar, it disappears with a poof.

Another way to customize the Finder's toolbar is either to select View → Customize Toolbar, or Option-⌘-click on the toolbar button. A sheet flops out of the Finder's titlebar, revealing a host of other buttons you can add to the toolbar. To add a new button, just drag the item to the toolbar and place it wherever you'd like. When you've finished configuring the toolbar to your liking, click Done.

The Action Menu

The Finder's Action menu (the one that looks like a little gear wheel), shown in Figure 21, is one of the marvels of the Finder.

Figure 21. The Finder's Action menu gives you lots of options for tasks that you'd otherwise have to go back up to the menu bar to use.

If you click on a file or folder in the Finder and then click on the Action menu, a pop-up menu appears, which lets you do any of the following:

- Create a **New Folder** within the selected folder or within the same folder if the item selected is a file.

- Create a **New Burnable Folder**, which can be burned to CD or DVD later without having to use Disk Utility (see Part V).

- **Open** the selected item. Files open in their associated application (for example, Word files open in Microsoft Word, HTML files open in Safari, etc.) and folders open in a new Finder window; if the selected item is an application icon, the application opens.

- **Move to Trash** moves the selected item to trash so you can delete (or recover) it later.

- Open the **Get Info** window to see details about the selected item.

- **Duplicate** the selected item. This creates an exact duplicate of the item you've selected and tacks on the word "copy" to its filename (for example, if you make a duplicate of *myfile.txt*, its copy of that file is named *myfile copy.txt*).

TIP

Another option for making a duplicate of a file is to first select the file in the Finder and then use the ⌘-D keyboard shortcut.

Keep in mind that this is much different than using the same keyboard shortcut within an Open or Save dialog box (which switches from its present disk location to the Desktop so you can open or save a file there).

- The **Make Alias** option lets you create an alias (sort of a shortcut or symbolic link) of the item, which you can then place elsewhere on your Mac.

For example, say you have a folder named Home Movies inside your Movies folder. In order to get to that folder, you need to open a Finder window, select Movies from the Sidebar (or from your Home folder), and then select the Home Movies folder. Wouldn't it be easier if you just had an icon for the Home Movies folder on your Desktop, which you could double-click to open the actual folder? If you select the Home Movies folder in the Finder, and select Make Alias, an alias of that folder is created there. Now all you need to do is drag that aliased folder to your Desktop and your life suddenly gets easier.

- **Create Archive** lets you create a zipped archive of the selected file or folder. This is particularly handy when you want to quickly create a Zip archive of only a few files within a folder.

  If you've only selected one file to zip, the Finder creates a *.zip* file, retaining the original filename (for example, if you select *myfile.txt* and select Create Archive, the zipped file is named *myfile.txt.zip*). However, if you select more than one file, the zipped file is given the generic name of *Archive.zip*; you'll need to change the name of the file if you want it to be something recognizable (such as *myworkfiles.zip*).

TIP

⌘-click the files you want to archive, then select Create Archive from the Action menu. To unzip an archive, just double-click the Zip file to unpack it in the Finder.

- **Copy** the selected item to the clipboard. If an item has been copied to the clipboard, a Paste option then becomes available in the Action item so you can paste a copy of the item in another location on your Mac.

- **Show View Options** is only available when you've selected an item in the Finder's Sidebar, but nothing in the View area. When selected, this opens a palette window, which you can use to adjust the settings for that particular Finder View. Once you've changed the View's settings, click the red close-window button to close the palette. Any future Finder windows of that View type will use the settings you've applied.

- The **Slideshow** option is available when you've selected one or more images. For example, if you select a bunch of JPEG images in your Pictures folder, you can click the Action menu, select Slideshow, and watch a slide show of the images, as shown in Figure 22.

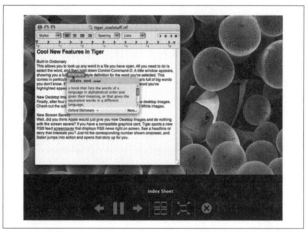

Figure 22. Tiger's slideshow feature (also available in Spotlight and Mail) offers a great way to preview images. Move your mouse to the bottom of the screen to use the controls (back, pause, forward, index sheet, full-screen, and quit).

- Finally, you'll see an × followed by a row of gumdrop-like colored dots at the very bottom of the Action menu. These are color **Labels**, which you can apply to any item you select in the Finder. (The × turns the Label off for the selected item.)

When you apply a Label to an item, the name of the item is colored with the color of your choice. Labels can be used for anything your little heart desires, from colorizing your hard drive to prioritizing project folders. Labels can even be assigned a name, using the Labels pane of the Finder's preferences (Finder → Preferences → Labels).

Searching from the Finder

As shown earlier in Figure 16, the Finder's toolbar sports a Search field, which was added to the Finder in Mac OS X 10.2 (Jaguar), replacing Sherlock's old system search functionality. And now with Tiger, Spotlight's been built-in to give you even greater search results. As soon as you start typing something into the Search field, Spotlight jumps into action and starts searching, as shown in Figure 23.

Figure 23. When searching from the Finder, Spotlight takes over and starts finding files as soon as you type something in.

As you can see from Figure 23, the Finder view area changes to show you the results. Along the top you'll see buttons for Servers, Computer, Home, Others, and a new Save button that lets you save your search as a Smart Folder. To add additional options, click the Add (+) button to the right of Save.

NOTE

If you find yourself doing the same search over and over again, you really should consider clicking that Save button. All you'll need to do the next time around is select the Smart Folder in the Finder's Sidebar, and your results instantly come into the Finder view.

Finder Tips

The following are some tips for working with the Finder:

Hide the Finder toolbar and Sidebar?
    View → Hide Toolbar (Option-⌘-T).

    Click on the transparent button in the upper-right corner of the titlebar.

Customize the Finder toolbar?
    Finder → View → Customize Toolbar.

    Option-⌘-click the toolbar button.

    Control-click within the toolbar and select Customize Toolbar from the context menu.

Show only the icons or text labels of items in the toolbar?
    View → Customize Toolbar → Show → select Icon & Text from the pull-down menu.

Locate a specific folder in the Finder?
    Go → Go to Folder (or Shift-⌘-G).

NOTE

You can use Shift-⌘-G to go to directories such as */usr* and */bin*, which are part of Mac OS X's Unix filesystem.

Search for hidden dot files on my system?

Open the Find dialog (File → Find, or ⌘-F). From the first pop-up menu, select Name, and in the field next to "contains," enter the word for which you'd like to search. In the next line, select Visibility from the pop-up menu and then select "invisible items" or "visible and invisible items" from the next pop-up menu.

NOTE

You can force the Finder to view Unix directories by using the Go → Go to Folder (Shift-⌘-G) option and entering a Unix filesystem path (such as */etc*).

Creating New Folders

Folders. Seems like a pretty simple concept, doesn't it? Well, now with Mac OS X Tiger, you have options for creating three different types of folders:

- Regular folders
- Smart Folders
- Burn Folders

Everybody's used to creating a folder; for this you either select File → New Folder or use the Shift-⌘-N keyboard shortcut in the Finder. But now with Tiger, you have the option to create Smart Folders and Burn Folders anywhere you'd like.

Smart Folders have been around since Panther, but they've been stuck in applications such as iTunes and iPhoto. To create a Smart Folder, select File → New Smart Folder (or Option-⌘-N). For an example of how to put Smart Folders to good use, see "Files and Folders" in Part VII.

Burn Folders offer a quick and easy way for you to burn files to CD or DVD. To create a Burn Folder, just select File →

New Burn Folder (there is no keyboard shortcut), give the folder a name, and then start dragging files to it. The files you place in the Burn Folder are actually aliased to the original file. To burn your Burn Folder to CD/DVD, just select the Burn Folder in the Finder, and then click the Burn button. For an example of how to use a Burn Folder, see "Files and Folders" in Part VII.

The Services Menu

The Services menu is available as a submenu in the Application menu of most Mac OS X applications. It allows the foreground application to invoke functions of other applications, usually while passing along user-selected text or objects to them.

The Service menu's contents depend on the applications installed on your Mac and the services they offer to other applications. When installed, some applications such as Mail, Safari, and BBEdit place entries in the Services menu. If an application provides more than one service, those items are placed into a submenu named after that application. For example, Mail offers two services, Send Selection and Send To, as shown in Figure 24.

With some text selected in a TextEdit document (as shown in Figure 24), select TextEdit (the Application menu) → Services → Mail → Send Selection. Mac OS X copies that text and places it in the body of a new message in Mail. Then all you need to do is enter the email address of the person to whom you want to send the text, and click on the Send button. (The Services → Mail → Send To option places the selected item in an email message's To field.)

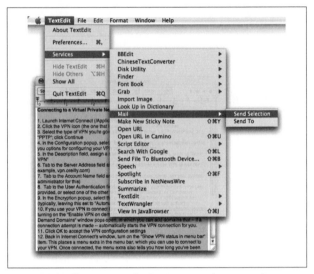

Figure 24. Mail's options in the Services menu let you send text selections in an email message.

NOTE

Some services also offer keyboard shortcuts, which makes it easy to send selected text to a Bluetooth device (Shift-⌘-B) or to create a new sticky note (Shift-⌘-Y).

Exposé

If you've ever wished for a quick way to get at your desktop, or just at the windows for a single application, Exposé is your answer. Exposé (shown in Figure 25) uses Quartz Extreme and OpenGL to make accessing windows—and your desktop—a dream come true.

Exposé runs in the background and is configurable through its System Preferences panel (System Preferences → Dash-

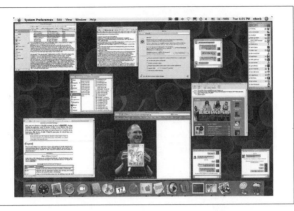

Figure 25. Exposé in action

board & Exposé). The keyboard shortcuts for Exposé are listed in Table 6.

Table 6. Keyboard shortcuts for Exposé

Key command	Description
F9	Spreads out all open windows so they're viewable on the desktop.
F10	Separates just the application windows (not including the Finder windows) so they're viewable on the desktop.
F11	Clears all of the windows away from the desktop so you can see what's there.

After using one of Exposé's keyboard shortcuts, you can either click on the window you'd like to bring forward or use the arrow keys on your keyboard to move around; to select a window, hit the Return key.

Using the Dashboard & Exposé preferences panel (System Preferences → Dashboard & Exposé), you can set Hot Corners for performing the actions of the function keys, or change the key settings to some other key combination. Hot Corners allow you to set the corners of your screen as special "hot" points, which invoke some action when you move your mouse there. For example, you could set the upper-left corner to enable Exposé's All Windows option, and the lower-left corner to Show Desktop, which scoots all open windows off-screen temporarily so you can see what's on the desktop.

Dashboard

One of the most talked-about additions for Mac OS X Tiger is Dashboard. The Dashboard offers a set of mini-applications, known as Widgets, which provide you with easy access to information when you need it. The beauty of Dashboard Widgets is that they're small, they don't take up very much of your Mac's system resources (memory and CPU power), and best of all, they're only in your face when you need them.

The Widgets that come pre-installed with Mac OS X Tiger include:

Address Book
 Provides an interface to the contacts stored in your Address Book application.

Calculator
 Works as a simple calculator for doing basic math..

Dictionary/Thesaurus
 Acts as either a dictionary or a thesaurus depending on which item you select in the Widget's "titlebar." To use this multi-function Widget, just select the desired func-tion, type a word into the Search field, and you'll soon see a definition of the word and/or a list of synonyms.

Flight Tracker
 Uses the web to help you track the progress of any flight on most major airlines around the world.

iCal
 Despite its name, only lets you view a simple calendar, showing you the date and a view of the current month.

Unfortunately, this Widget does not pull in information from your iCal calendars or to-do lists.

iTunes

When iTunes is running, provides a very slick interface for operating iTunes. The interface for the iTunes Widget is very similar to that for the DVD Player application (*/Applications*).

Stickies

Lets you create Stickies notes, which you can use to quickly get at information you need. These Stickies are separate from those you create with Mac OS X's Stickies application (*/Applications*), and, unlike those Stickies, cannot contain images.

Stocks

Pulls current stock information from Quote.com's web services, providing you with a 20-minute-delayed ticker. To add a stock symbol for this Widget to track, click on the info icon ("i") in the lower-right corner.

Tile Game

Scrambles up a picture of a Tiger; it's your job to move the individual tiles around to put the picture back in its original state. To play this game, click one of the tiles to shuffle the tiles of the puzzle, click again to stop the tiles from shuffling, and then click a tile next to the empty space to move that tile into the empty space. Repeat until you put the puzzle back together again.

Translator

Translates words and phrases. Need to find out how to say "Where is the bathroom?" in Spanish? Look no further than the Translator Widget. Just type in the word (or words) you want to search for, then select the From and To languages from the pop-up menus. The translation instantly appears in the To field.

Unit Converter

Quickly converts various units of measure from one to another. This multi-function Widget includes a pop-up menu that lets you select Area, Energy, Temperature, Time, Length, Weight, Speed, Pressure, Power, or Volume. Each type lets you select From and To conversion types, so feel free to play around with these. For example, if you've ever wondered how many seconds there are in a year, you can find the answer here.

Weather

Uses information it gathers from AccuWeather.com's web services to provide you with up-to-date weather information for any city in the United States, as well as for some cities in other countries.

World Clock

Tells you what time it is where you live, or, if you're using additional clock Widgets, tells you the time elsewhere in the world. Between the hours of 6 a.m. and 6 p.m., the face is white, while between 6 p.m. and 6 a.m., the face is set to black. This is a quick way for you to tell if it's daytime or nighttime in the place for which the clock is set.

Yellow Pages

Finds local businesses and organizations. Need to find a roofing company or a professional dog-walking service in your area? Let the Yellow Pages Widget "do the walking" for you.

Now that you know what's available to you—Widget-wise—it's time to see how these things work.

Viewing the Dashboard

There are three ways you can bring Dashboard's Widgets into view:

- Click on Dashboard's icon in the Dock
- Press the F12 key (or Fn-F12 if you use a PowerBook or iBook)

Finding More Widgets

It won't take long before you're addicted to the Dashboard. You'll find lots of great uses for it, such as relying on the Dashboard's Clock Widget to get your time instead of taking up valuable space in the menu bar with the clock menu extra. But what if you want more? Where can you turn to find more Widgets?

If you look at Figure 27, you'll notice another button, labeled "More Widgets," off to the right, just above Dashboard's dock. When you click this button, you're taken to Apple's own Dashboard web site, located at *http://www.apple.com/macosx/dashboard*. There you'll not only find more Widgets you can download and install on your Mac (save them to */Library/Widgets*), but you'll also find tutorials on how to build your own Dashboard Widget.

If Apple's site isn't enough for you, there's always The Dashboarder (*http://www.thedashboarder.com*), which has been around ever since Apple revealed the Dashboard at their Worldwide Developer's Conference (WWDC) in June 2004. The Dashboarder offers a variety of Widgets, from Tetris-like games to system utilities for checking the status of your CPU. Another site you can try is WidgetTracker (*http://www.widgettracker.com*).

And if you're a whiz at web design, you can employ your own HTML, CSS, and JavaScript skills to build your own Dashboard Widget. To find out more information about building and designing Dashboard Widgets, take a read through Apple's Dashboard documentation, located at *http://developer.apple.com*.

- Move your mouse to Dashboard's Hot Corner (if you've set that up in System Preferences → Dashboard & Exposé → Dashboard → Hot Corners)

When you do, any previously running Dashboard Widgets come into view, as shown in Figure 26.

Figure 26. When you hit the F12 key, Dashboard's Widgets pop into view, giving you quick access to the information or services they provide.

As previously mentioned, there are only a couple of keyboard shortcuts you can use to get at the Dashboard. Table 7 has a complete list of them.

Table 7. Dashboard's keyboard shortcuts

Key command	Description
F12 (or Fn-F12 with laptops)	Brings the Dashboard into view; hit this key again and the Dashboard goes away.
Shift-F12 (or Shift-Fn-F12 with laptops)	Similar to using F12, except the Shift key brings the Dashboard into/out of view slowly (very slowly).

If you look closely at Figure 26, you'll notice a little circle with a plus sign (+) inside at your display's lower-left corner. When you click this icon, your screen changes as Mac OS X Tiger's full Dashboard pops into view along the bottom as its own "dock" (as shown in Figure 27).

On either side of the Dashboard's dock, you'll see little arrows pointing left and right, respectively. This lets you know that there are more Widgets to view and use. Just click

Figure 27. Dashboard's dock gives you quick access to other Widgets installed on your Mac.

on one of these "scroller" arrows, and a new set of Widgets appears.

To use one of the other Widgets, just click the one you need to pop it into view, or click-and-drag the Widget's icon from Dashboard's dock. This lets you drag the Widget to a screen location of your choice. To close a Widget (make it slip back down into Dashboard's dock), just move your mouse over it, and a circled × appears in the upper-left corner of the Widget. Click this × and the Widget goes away.

Widget Preferences

One of the cool things about Dashboard's Widgets is that you can have multiple "versions" of the same Widget open at a time, just as you can have more than one Finder or Word document window open at any time. For example, let's say you're using the Weather Widget to monitor the six-day weather forecast where you live, but you also want to see what the weather is going to be like where your friend Scott is, in Chicago. You could always change the Widget's preferences to view the weather for Chicago and then change it back to your own city, but that just seems silly.

Instead, you can click again on the Weather Widget's icon in Dashboard's dock to pop open another Widget. To change the preferences for that Widget so it tracks the weather in Chicago, move your mouse to the lower-right corner of the Weather Widget's window. You'll see a little "i" (information) icon appear; click this. The Widget "flips" over, revealing a field where you can set that window's preferences. You can either type in the City and State, or enter the ZIP Code for the Widget, as shown in Figure 28.

Figure 28. To select another location in the Weather Widget's preferences, just type in the City and State, or the ZIP Code, and click Done.

Now when you press the F12 key to bring the Dashboard to the front, you'll see the weather report for both cities in two separate Weather Widgets, as shown in Figure 29.

Spotlight

One of the most anticipated new features of Mac OS X Tiger is Spotlight. Spotlight combs through each and every file on

Figure 29. Same Widget, two different weather reports

your computer and creates an index not only of the file-
names, but also of *every single word inside the files*, including
words it finds tucked inside PDF documents.

Immediately after you install Mac OS X Tiger, whenever you
log in to your account, and whenever you add or change or
delete a file on your system, Spotlight jumps into action and
collects information known as *metadata* about each and
every file. And if you've attached an external FireWire drive
to your Mac, Spotlight indexes all of the information on that
drive as well.

The metadata collected by Spotlight includes information
about the file—the date it was created or changed, where it's
located in the filesystem, etc.—as well as information about

the words Spotlight finds inside the file. This makes Spotlight truly amazing, because you can do keyword searches and get results for any type of file found on your system.

NOTE

Spotlight does not collect metadata for Unix files found at the system level; it only indexes files you access through the Aqua interface. If you're a Unix-head and you know what somebody means when they refer to "et-cee files" (files stored in the /etc directory), then you probably already know how to search through files using *find*, *locate*, or *grep*.

Now that you know what Spotlight is and a little about how it works, let's put it into action and *find* something.

Searching with Spotlight

To search with Spotlight, you can either click on the little blue magnifying glass, located at the far-right edge of the menu bar, or you can hit ⌘-Space to pop open Spotlight's search field, shown in Figure 30. Best of all, you can use that keyboard shortcut from within any application, which makes it really easy for you, since you don't have to switch over to the Finder to search for something.

Figure 30. Spotlight's search field appears beneath the menu bar, attached to the blue Spotlight icon, as its own menu.

To search for something, just type in a word or series of words (known as a *string*), as shown in Figure 31. Spotlight doesn't wait for you to finish typing to begin its metadata search; it starts searching as soon as you type the first character.

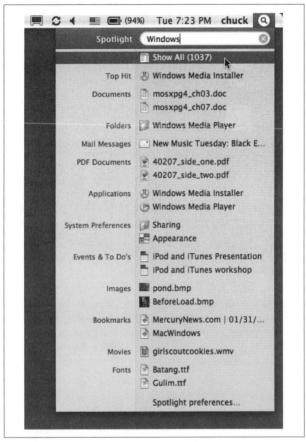

Figure 31. After you type in a word to search for, Spotlight displays its top finds by category.

As you can see from Figure 31, Spotlight categorizes the search results right beneath its search field. This is very convenient because you don't have to sort through an alphabetical list of results; instead, you can see instantly whether the search term is in a Word or PDF file, or even buried deep within some iChat message.

Among Spotlight's search results, you'll notice three items that stand out—two at the top of the window and one at the bottom; everything in between relates to your search.

Show All (#)
> The # shown in parentheses is the number of items Spotlight finds that match your search criteria.

Top Hit
> Of all the files or folders on your Mac, Spotlight thinks the item shown here is the one for which you're looking. This may or may not be the correct item, though, so think twice before clicking on it.

TIP

To quickly select the Top Hit in Spotlight's results, press the ⌘ key.

Spotlight preferences...
> Click this item and Spotlight's preferences panel opens in System Preferences. Use this window to configure either Spotlight's search activities or even the keyboard shortcuts you use to access Spotlight's search field or window (we'll get to that in a sec).

If you see the file you're looking for in Spotlight's search results, all you need to do to open the file is bring the mouse down and click the item once. However, if you can't find the file you're looking for and you know it should be there, you can choose the Show All option to open the Spotlight window (see Figure 32). Spotlight's window gives you a detailed, categorized view of everything that matches your search results.

Spotlight's search window (which you can open anytime with its keyboard shortcut, Option-⌘-Space) breaks down

---

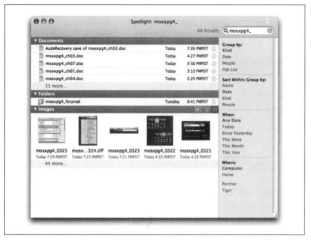

Figure 32. Spotlight's window lets you sift through the search results further, helping you find exactly the thing for which you're looking.

the search results and categorizes them for you. Click the disclosure triangle to open/collapse categories, or the "i" (info) button to reveal information about a particular file. Depending on the type of files found, you'll also see a few icons at the right edge of the blue category bars. These icons allow you to change the way in which the items found are displayed. For example:

- If the category is Images, you'll see a Play button, which, when pressed, plays the images as a slideshow (see Figure 22 earlier).

- The List button, which looks like a bunch of horizontal lines, displays the search results as a list (this is the default for most items, including the Documents category, shown in Figure 32).

- When pressed, the Icon button shows you a thumbnail preview for any image files that show up in the search results. Spotlight even offers previews for Photoshop files (ending with a *.psd* file extension) in this list, making it really easy for you to find the image you're looking for without having to open the file.

Use the bar on the right of Spotlight's window to help refine your search. For example, if you wanted to see only those files that have been changed in the last week, go to the When category and select "This Week." Spotlight then checks the dates of all the files in your search, pulls forward those that have been worked on in the last seven days, and displays them in the window to the left.

Spotlight's Preferences

As previously noted, Spotlight has its own preference panel, which is located within the System Preferences application. Use Spotlight's preference panel to:

- Select the order in which Spotlight categorizes its search results. For example, if you know you'll mostly be searching for something within a document, you can click on the Documents item and drag it to the top of the list.

- Change the keyboard shortcut for accessing the Spotlight menu; by default, this is set to ⌘-Space.

- Change the keyboard shortcut for accessing Spotlight's window; by default, this is set to Option-⌘-Space.

You'll also notice that there's a Privacy tab in Spotlight's preference panel. Use this tab to choose items you don't want Spotlight to index and search through. For example, if you don't want Spotlight to display images in your iPhoto Library, click the Add button (+) and choose your Pictures folder on the sheet that appears.

Get Info and File Permissions

Get Info gives you access to all sorts of information about the files, directories, and applications on your system. To view the information for an item, click on its icon in the Finder

---

and either go to File → Get Info or use the keyboard shortcut ⌘-I. The Get Info window has six different panes that each offer different kinds of information about the file. To reveal the content of one of these items, click on its disclosure triangle to expand the pane. The panes of the Get Info window include the following:

Spotlight Comments

Here you'll find an empty text field in which you can type additional information about the file (such as "This is Part III for the Mac OS X Tiger Pocket Guide," or "This article is for the Mac DevCenter"). The next time Spotlight indexes the files on your system, it picks up the information you entered in these fields and uses that as additional metadata for the file.

General

This tells you the basics about the file, including its kind, its size, where it's located in the filesystem, and when it was created and last modified. If you are looking at the Info for a file, you will see two checkboxes in the General section: Stationary Pad and Locked. If you enable these options, the file can be used as a template or is made read-only, respectively.

More Info

For folders and hard drives (including partitions and disk images), the More Info box displays the date and time the item was last opened. For files, the same information is displayed; however, Word files display the author (or creator) of the file, and image files display information such as the image's dimensions (in pixels) and its color space (such as RGB, CMYK, or Gray for grayscale images).

Name & Extension

This displays a text box with the name of the file or directory.

Open with

> This option is available only if you select a file (i.e., not a folder or an application). Here you can specify which application opens this file or all similar files.

Preview

> Depending on the file type, you can preview the contents of the file here (this also works for playing sounds and QuickTime movies).

Ownership & Permissions

> This displays the name of the owner and the name of the group to which the file belongs. It also allows you to set access privileges to that file for the Owner, Group, and Others on the system.

The Get Info window for applications includes the General Information, Name & Extension, and Ownership & Permissions options mentioned previously (although the Ownership & Permissions options are disabled by default), as well as one or both of the following options:

Languages

> This shows the languages the application supports. The languages are displayed with checkboxes next to them. To make an application run faster, turn off the languages you don't need by unchecking the box.

Plug-ins

> If applicable, this lists the available plug-ins for the application. For example, iMovie and iPhoto's Get Info windows have a Plug-ins section.

NOTE

Noticeably missing from a Mac OS X application's Get Info window is the Memory option. Because memory for applications is assigned dynamically by virtual memory, you no longer have to specify how much memory an application requires. However, if you use Get Info on a Mac OS 9 application, the Memory option is available.

PART IV

System Preferences

Before Mac OS X came along, you'd have to fumble through the Control Panels to set up your Mac, but with Mac OS X, Apple has made all these "panels" self-contained in the System Preferences application. When you want to set up your Mac just for you, System Preferences is the application you're looking for. To launch the System Preferences application, simply click on the light-switch icon in the Dock, and the window shown in Figure 33 appears.

Figure 33. The System Preferences window

System Preferences is home to a series of preference panels you use for configuring your Mac. For example, if you wanted to select Mac OS X Tiger's new Apple News screensaver, you would launch System Preferences by clicking its icon in the Dock, and then click Desktop & Screen Saver. This opens the preference panel, shown in Figure 34. It has two tabbed "panes," aptly named Desktop and Screen Saver. To change the settings for your screensaver, click the tab for the Screen Saver pane, then select a screensaver from the list on the lefthand side of the window.

Figure 34. The Desktop & Screen Saver preference panel

As you may have noticed in Figure 33, the System Preferences are separated into four categories: Personal, Hardware, Internet & Network, and System. When you click one of the icons, the window changes to reflect that particular panel's settings. To go back to the main view, click the Show All button (View → Show All Preferences, or use the keyboard shortcut, ⌘-L). You can also select View → Organize

---

Alphabetically; this menu option changes the view of the System Preferences window to that shown in Figure 35.

Figure 35. The System Preferences, listed alphabetically

When you've completed setting your Mac's preferences, you can quit System Preferences by selecting System Preferences → Quit (⌘-Q), or by simply closing the System Preferences window using Window → Close (⌘-W).

NOTE

Some of the System Preferences panels require administrator privileges. If you attempt to change a setting and are asked for a password, try using the password you used to log in to the computer. If that doesn't work, contact your system administrator for assistance.

Searching for Preferences

Of the many new features added for Tiger, some of the best show up here in System Preferences. If you take a close look at the toolbar (along the top of the System Preferences window), you'll notice a new feature: a search field. Now, for some Mac users, the thought of having a search field in System Preferences might seem odd, but if you have only an idea of what it is you want to do, this new field quickly comes to the rescue.

To conduct a search, either click in the search field in the toolbar, or use the standard Mac keyboard shortcut for "find," ⌘-F. For example, if you're a Windows user who is new to the Mac, you might not be familiar yet with all the Mac lingo. So, when you go to System Preferences and want to set a new desktop image, you might still be thinking of "wallpaper." To help find what you're looking for, start typing "wallpaper" in System Preferences' search field, as shown in Figure 36.

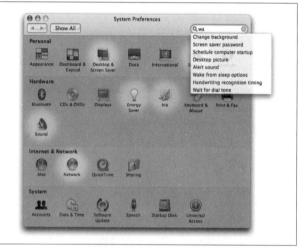

Figure 36. Use the search field in Tiger's System Preferences application to quickly find the right preference panel for configuring your Mac.

In this case, since you're looking for "wallpaper," you'll see that "Desktop picture" shows up as one of the options in

System Preferences' search results. To open this panel, simply move your mouse down and click on "Desktop picture." The circle of light (a spotlight; cute, huh?) flashes twice on the Desktop & Screen Saver panel and opens it up in the window.

NOTE

You can also use the arrow keys to highlight items in System Preferences' search results. This can be somewhat entertaining, as pressing the Down or Up arrow keys focuses the Spotlight on the corresponding panel, giving you a Christmas tree–like effect as the glow moves around the window. Go on, give it a try; you know you want to.

System Preferences Overview

The next four sections provide an overview of the controls found in the System Preferences. For additional information on how to use the System Preferences panels to configure your system, see Part VII.

Personal

These items control the general look and feel of the Aqua interface.

Appearance
When selected, this panel, which used to be the General panel in Jaguar, specifies the colors used for buttons and menu items, the location of scrollbar arrows (top and bottom, or together, known as "Smart Scrolling" in Mac OS 9), and how a click in the scrollbar will be interpreted (scroll down one page or scroll to that location in the document). Here, you can specify the number of recent items to be remembered and listed in the → Recent Items menu for applications and documents, as

---

well as determine which font-smoothing style and size is best for your type of display.

Dashboard & Exposé

This preference panel lets you configure the settings for Dashboard and Exposé's Hot Corners. For more information on using Dashboard and Exposé, or to learn more about what Hot Corners are, see the "Dashboard" and "Exposé" sections in Part III.

Desktop & Screen Saver

This panel has two panes, one you can use to set the background image for your desktop, and the other to select your screensaver. The Desktop pane lets you choose the pattern, image, or color of your desktop. If you click on the checkbox next to "Change picture" at the bottom of the window, the desktop picture changes automatically based on the timing you select in the pull-down menu.

The Screen Saver pane lets you select one of Mac OS X's default screensaver modules. Here, you can set the amount of time your system must be inactive before the screensaver kicks in, require a password to turn off the screensaver, and specify Hot Corners for enabling/disabling the screensaver. For example, you could set the upper-right corner of your display to start the screensaver and the lower-right corner to prevent the screensaver from turning on if your mouse is located there.

NOTE

If you have a .Mac account, you can also choose from the .Mac Screen Effects or subscribe to another .Mac member's public slide show. To do this, click on the Configure button and enter the member's username (for example, *chuckdude*).

Dock

This is one of the ways you can configure your Dock (another is by going to ■ → Dock → Dock Preferences). See "Using and Configuring the Dock," in Part III, for details on the Dock.

International

This is used to set the languages supported by your system. The language you specify during the installation process will be the default. Also found here are controls to format the date, time, numbers, and currency, as well as the keyboard layout to be used for a country and its language.

If you select more than one language in the tabbed Input Menu pane, a menu extra appears in the menu bar showing flags of the countries whose languages are supported on your system.

NOTE

Earlier versions of Mac OS X let you use ⌘-Space to toggle between keyboard languages in the Input Menu. However, Tiger uses ⌘-Space to open and close Spotlight's search field. If you want to set a keyboard shortcut for the Input Menu so you can switch from U.S. English to Canadian English (trust me, it's an option), use the Keyboard Shortcuts pane in the Keyboard & Mouse preference pane.

Security

This panel lets you set up a FileVault for your Home folder by encrypting its contents. FileVault uses Kerberos authentication to encrypt and decrypt files automatically. To enable FileVault, you'll need to set the master password, and then click the Turn on FileVault button. After entering your login password (not the master password you've just set), you can turn on FileVault protection. All of the files in your Home folder are encrypted with your login password. This protects your files from being accessed by other users on your computer, or from some-one who might boot your Mac into Target Mode (see Table 1 in Part II) with malicious intent. When FileVault finishes encrypting your files, you are required to log back in, after which you'll notice that the icon for your Home folder in the Finder has changed from a friendly-looking house to one that looks like an imposing metallic safe.

The Security panel also has checkboxes at the bottom with options for requiring a password when waking your computer from sleep or screensaver mode, disabling automatic login, and logging out automatically if your Mac has been inactive for a certain amount of time.

Spotlight

This panel gives you added control when using Spot-light. Use the Search Results pane to configure the order in which Spotlight displays its results. You can uncheck items you don't want displayed in the search results, or you can drag them around in the list. For example, if you want the contacts in your Address Book to appear first, simply click on Contacts and drag it to the top of the list; the other items move down in the chain. If there are any folders or disks you don't want Spotlight to index, use the Privacy pane.

The two checkboxes at the bottom (and their corre-sponding pop-up menus) let you configure the keyboard shortcuts used to open Spotlight's search field in the menu bar (set to ⌘-Space by default) as well as the Spot-light window (set to Option-⌘-Space by default).

Hardware

These panels are used to control the settings for the devices connected to your computer.

Bluetooth

This panel allows you to configure the settings for using Bluetooth to exchange files with other users and to synchronize data between your computer and other devices, such as cellular phones and PDAs. This item appears only if you have a Bluetooth-enabled Mac (such as the Mac mini or a PowerBook) or a Bluetooth dongle (such as the one Apple promotes from D-Link) inserted into one of the USB slots.

CDs & DVDs

The items in the CDs & DVDs panel all share the same basic interface: a pull-down menu that lets you choose what the Mac does when it mounts various kinds of discs. You can choose to have it simply open the new media volume as a Finder window, launch an appropriate application (such as iTunes for music CDs and Disk Copy for blank discs), run a script, or prompt you to take some other action.

Displays

This panel lets you set your monitor's resolution and color-depth (256, thousands, or millions of colors). It also has an option to include a monitor menu extra in the menu bar, as well as a slider control to set your monitor's brightness. If you have more than one monitor connected to your system, clicking on the Detect Displays button allows you to specify settings for each display.

NOTE

If you use a CRT display, the Displays panel also offers a Rotate pop-up menu, which lets you rotate the display (clockwise) 90 degrees at a time. For example, select 180 and watch your display flip upside-down. Of course, this makes it a little more difficult to use your mouse, but it sure looks goofy. (The Rotate feature is not available on laptop computers, such as the iBook or PowerBook.)

Energy Saver

This panel is used to set the auto-sleep settings for your computer. Here, you can specify the amount of time your system must be idle before Energy Saver puts your monitor, hard drive, or the entire system to sleep.

PowerBook and iBook users will also see two pull-down menus at the top of this panel. The first pull-down menu, Settings for, gives you options for controlling the Energy Saver settings for when you're plugged in (Power Adapter) or when you're operating on battery (Battery). The second, Optimization, lets you either select from four preset options or specify custom settings.

Ink

This item appears only if you have a graphics tablet (such as a Wacom tablet) connected to your system. Ink controls how handwritten text is handled by the InkPad. The Gestures tab includes pen strokes for invoking commands such as Undo, Cut, Copy, Paste, insert a space or carriage return (Vertical Space), and more.

Keyboard & Mouse

This panel contains the following four panes:

Keyboard

This pane controls the repeat rate, or the rate at which a key repeats when you depress it and hold it down. You can specify the speed of the repeat (from slow to fast) and the delay between the time the key is first depressed until the repeat option kicks in (from long to short). If you select the Off option for Delay Until Repeat, the repeat feature will be disabled entirely.

Mouse (or Trackpad, if you have a PowerBook or iBook)

This pane lets you specify the mouse's Tracking Speed as well as the delay between double-clicks. If you are using an iBook or PowerBook, the Mouse preferences panel will have an additional section for setting the controls for your Trackpad.

Bluetooth

This pane lets you configure the settings for Apple's Bluetooth keyboard and mouse, if you have them. The Mouse and Keyboard sections have indicators to show the battery level for each device.

Keyboard Shortcuts

This pane lists the various keyboard shortcuts you can use on your Mac. You can also add, remove, or change the shortcuts to suit your needs.

At the bottom of this window are two radio buttons for controlling Full Keyboard Access, one of the many accessibility features built into Mac OS X Tiger. Full Keyboard Access is always on in Mac OS X Tiger, which means anyone can use their keyboard to perform all the functions of the mouse, without ever having to use the mouse—you use the keys on your keyboard instead. Full Keyboard Access lets you use the Tab key to set the keyboard focus to either "Text boxes and lists only" or "All controls" (the default setting). For example, with "Text boxes and lists only" selected, you use the Tab key to move between Full Keyboard Access's key combinations listed in Table 8.

Table 8. Full Keyboard Access's key combinations

Function keys	Description
Control-F1	Enable/disable keyboard access.
Control-F2	Control the menu bar.
Control-F3	Control the Dock.
Control-F4	Activate the window or the first window behind it.
Control-F5	Control an application's toolbar.
Control-F6	Control an application's utility window (or palette).
Control-F7	Highlight either text input fields and lists, or any window control (used for windows and dialogs).
Control-F8	Move the focus to the status menus at the right side of the menu bar.

Table 8. Full Keyboard Access's key combinations (continued)

Function keys	Description
Esc	Return control to the mouse, disabling the Control-Fx key combination.
Spacebar	Perform the function of a mouse click.

NOTE

If you are using an iBook or PowerBook, you need to use Control plus the *fn* key, along with the Function or Letter key for keyboard access, in order to perform the commands in Table 8; for example, Control-fn-F2 to access menus. The *fn* key is at the bottom-left corner of your keyboard, to the left of the Control key (and below the Shift key).

Print & Fax

    This panel is used to configure printers and set up your Mac to accept faxes. From the Faxing pane, you can opt to have incoming faxes saved to a directory, emailed to you, or sent to a printer. Use the Sharing tab to set up printer and fax sharing, which lets other Macs on your network use the printer connected to your Mac.

Sound

    This panel offers two panes—one for configuring Alert sounds, and another for sound Output (e.g., speakers). The Alerts pane has an option for including a volume control slider in the menu bar.

Internet & Network

The following panels are used to control your Mac's settings for connecting to other computers.

.Mac

    This panel has four tabbed panes, Account, Sync, iDisk, and Advanced, which allow you to configure the settings for your .Mac account, see how much space is available on your iDisk, or set up Tiger's .Mac Sync features. You can also share your synchronized data with other Macs, using the new Advanced pane.

NOTE

In earlier versions of Mac OS X, you would use iSync to synchronize your data from your Mac to .Mac; however, with Tiger, iSync no longer works with your .Mac account. Instead, you'll need to use the Sync pane.

Network

This panel lets you configure your settings for dial-up, Ethernet, AirPort, and Bluetooth networking, including enabling/disabling AppleTalk. For details on how to configure these settings, see Part VII.

QuickTime

This panel lets you configure QuickTime's settings for playing back movies and music. If you've purchased a license for QuickTime Pro, click on the Registration button to enter the registration number.

Sharing

This panel lets you set the name of your computer and your Bonjour name. The lower portion of the Sharing panel has three tabbed panes:

Services

This pane allows you to turn on file, web, and printer sharing, control FTP access to your machine, and allow users of other computers to log into your machine remotely via SSH. The option to allow your computer's spare processor cycles to be used with Xgrid is new for Tiger. When turned on, Xgrid controllers can send tasks to your Mac to be performed in the background, using only the available processor resources.

Firewall
> This pane allows you to restrict people from the out-side world from gaining access to your machine through its various ports and services. The services you turn on in the Services pane control the enabled services in the Firewall pane. For example, if you turn on Personal File Sharing in the Services pane, the checkbox next to Personal Fire Sharing will be checked in the Firewall pane. By default, the firewall is turned off.

Internet
> This pane allows you to share your Internet connec-tion with other computers via AirPort or built-in Ethernet.

System

The items in the System panel allow you to configure a vari-ety of settings for your computer:

Accounts
> As the name implies, this panel is used to add and remove users and to make changes to their identities and passwords.

NOTE

If you have administrator privileges, you can also specify Parental Controls for a non-administrator's account for doing things such as removing items from the Dock, us-ing the System Preferences, changing passwords, burning CDs or DVDs, and even restricting which applications and utilities are available to the user. For more informa-tion, see "Parental Controls" in Part II.

Classic
> This panel is used to start, stop, and restart the Classic environment.

Date & Time

This panel is used to set the date, time, and time zone for your system, specify a network time server, and specify how (or whether) the date and time appears in the menu bar.

TIP

Want more space in your menu bar? Turn off the menu bar clock by unchecking the box next to "Show the date and time" in the Date & Time → Clock preference pane in System Preferences. Since you have Dashboard at your disposal, whenever you need to know what time it is, just hit F12, look at Dashboard's World Clock Widget, and then hit the F12 key again to make the clock (and all the other Widgets you have open) go away.

Software Update

As with Mac OS 9, this panel is used to check for updates to your Mac OS X system. You can check for updates manually (i.e., when you want to, or when you learn of an available update) or automatically (daily, weekly, or monthly). When an update is found, you are prompted to specify which updates will be downloaded and installed on your system.

If you enable the "Download important updates in the background" checkbox, Software Update automatically downloads and installs important updates, such as Security Updates.

NOTE

You can also launch Software Update from the Apple menu (🍎) by selecting the Software Update menu item.

Speech

This panel is used to turn on and configure speech recognition, specify a default voice for applications that speak text, and specify whether items in the user interface (such as alert messages or the text in menus) will be spoken.

Startup Disk

This panel is used to specify the hard drive or partition that your Mac uses to boot into Mac OS X. With Tiger, you can also specify a Network Startup disk if your computer is configured or set up via NetBoot from Mac OS X Server. Tiger's Startup Disk panel also features a Target Disk Mode button, which, when clicked, restarts your Mac and allows you to mount its hard drive as a FireWire drive on another Mac.

Universal Access

This panel provides support for people with disabilities. It features two panes for people who have problems Seeing or Hearing, and two more panes for those who find it difficult to use a Keyboard or Mouse. The Universal Access panel also lets you turn VoiceOver (new to Tiger) on or off, and includes a button that opens the VoiceOver Utility (*/Applications/Utilities*).

NOTE

One thing you'll notice quickly is that all the text labels for the user interface elements in the Universal Access panel are spoken using the voice you've specified in the Speech panel.

To quit the System Preferences application, you can use either ⌘-Q or ⌘-W. (Yes, closing the System Preferences window also quits the application.)

PART V

Applications and Utilities

What good is a computer without programs to run on it? Apple has included a set of native applications and utilities for Mac OS X, including the famous suite of iApps (iCal, iChat, iSync, and iTunes), along with a bunch of utilities to help you monitor and set up additional gear for your Mac.

There are applications for things such as viewing and printing PostScript and PDF files, basic word processing, sending and receiving email, and creating movies, as well as utilities to help you manage your system.

Use the Finder to locate the applications (*/Applications*) and utilities (*/Applications/Utilities*) on your system. You can quickly go to the Applications folder either by clicking on the Applications icon in the Sidebar or by using the Shift-⌘-A keyboard shortcut. If you want to be able to get to the Utilities folder quickly, you might consider dragging the Utilities folder icon to the Finder's Sidebar, or instead using its keyboard shortcut, Shift-⌘-U.

Applications

Following is a list of the programs found in the Applications directory:

Address Book
> This is a database program you can use to store contact information for your friends and colleagues.

AppleScript

This folder contains all the tools necessary for writing AppleScripts. AppleScript is an "English-like" scripting language native to the Mac, which you can use to help automate tasks, such as renaming a bunch of files or applying a Photoshop filter to a group of graphics you need for your web site. Inside the AppleScript folder you'll find the following items:

AppleScript Utility

This little program lets you choose a script editor (which is set to Mac OS X's Script Editor by default), lets you turn on GUI scripting (requires an administrator's password), and set up Folder Actions. It also offers an option for turning on the Script Menu for the menu bar.

Folder Actions Setup

This program lets you turn on Folder Actions and, once they're enabled, allows you to specify and track folders that have a Folder Action script applied to them.

Script Editor

The Script Editor is the application with which you'll create your AppleScripts.

You'll also see an alias to the Example Scripts folder (you'll know it's an alias because the folder icon has a little arrow on it), which is located in the main Library folder on your hard drive (Macintosh HD → Library).

Automator

New for Tiger, Automator is the killer app for users who need to automate processes, such as renaming a bunch of files in a folder, or converting images for your web site from PNGs to JPEGs. To use Automator, first select the application you want to control, then find an Action you want it to perform and drag that to the Workflow area. Need the Finder to hand off a process to Preview or iPhoto? No problem, there are Actions for those applications, too.

Calculator

The Calculator is a fully functional scientific calculator. Calculator also has a Paper Tape sheet that allows you to view the math functions, which you can then copy and paste into another document window.

Chess

The Chess program is based on GNU Chess. Apple has packaged this Unix-based chess game with a Cocoa interface and 3D game pieces.

Dashboard

Like the Finder, the Dashboard application is always running on your Mac. Dashboard offers you a set of "Widgets" that you can use to check the time or weather, see how your stock portfolio is doing, or check your friend's flight status, to name a few. See the "Dashboard" section in Part III for an overview of the Dashboard Widgets that come with Mac OS X Tiger.

NOTE

As with Automator, Apple has created a special Dashboard Center on their site to provide users with additional Widgets. Visit the site at *http://sww.apple.com/macosx/ dashboard*.

Dictionary

This application is very similar to the Dashboard's Dictionary Widget, mentioned in Part III in the "Dashboard" section. Use Dictionary to find the correct spelling and/or definition of a word that's stumping you. The Dictionary also features a built-in Thesaurus, so you can look up alternatives for a word you might be overusing.

DVD Player

You can use this application to view DVD movies on your Mac. If your hardware natively supports DVD playback, the DVD Player is installed.

Font Book

The Font Book application offers an intuitive way to pre-view the fonts on your Mac, as well as the ability to create font collections.

iCal

iCal is a calendaring application (similar to Entourage, if you're a Windows convert) that allows you to manage and publish your calendar to any WebDAV-enabled server (including your .Mac account). You can also subscribe to other calendars (such as a listing of holidays, the schedule for your favorite sports team, or another user's calendar).

iChat

iChat allows you to chat with other .Mac members, AOL Instant Messenger (AIM) users, and, new for Tiger, Jabber users as well. iChat also supports messaging via Bonjour for dynamically finding iChat users on your local network. The new version of iChat for Tiger allows you to video chat with up to 3 other people and audio chat with up to 10.

NOTE

Tiger's 4-way video chat and 10-way audio chat come with a price; there are specific system requirements for using these features. For an overview of iChat AV's exact system requirements, see *http://docs.info.apple.com/article.html?artnum=301050*. If your system isn't powerful enough, you won't be able to take advantage of these new features.

If you have an iSight camera, you can also use iChat for video conferencing over the Internet. To learn more about iSight, visit Apple's web site at *http://www.apple.com/isight*.

Image Capture

This program can be used to download pictures and video from a digital camera to your Mac. You can share input devices such as digital cameras and scanners attached to your Mac with other users on a network. To enable device sharing, go to Image Capture → Preferences (or ⌘-,) → Sharing, then click on the checkbox next to "Share my devices."

Internet Connect

This application is used for connecting to the Internet or to another computer via a dial-up modem or AirPort connection. You can use Internet Connect to connect your Mac to a Virtual Private Network (VPN) via File → New VPN Connection. In Panther, Internet Connect supports PPTP (Point-to-Point Tunneling Protocol) and L2TP (Layer 2 Tunneling Protocol) over IPSec for connecting to a VPN.

Internet Connect shows your current dial-up status and settings (as configured in the Network pane of your System Preferences) and provides a Connect/Disconnect button for opening or closing a connection.

iSync

iSync can be used to synchronize data—contact information from your Address Book, your iCal calendars, music, etc.—from your computer to another device such as a cellular phone, PDA, iPod, or another computer.

NOTE

As of Mac OS X Tiger, iSync no longer works for synchronizing your data to your .Mac account. Instead, you'll need to use the .Mac preference panel's Sync pane (System Preferences → .Mac → Sync).

---

iTunes

iTunes can be used to play CDs, listen to Internet radio stations, import (rip) music from CDs, burn CDs from music you've collected, and store and play MP3 files. If you have an iPod, you can use iTunes to synchronize your MP3 music files.

iTunes also serves as the virtual storefront for the iTunes Music Store (ITMS). If you have an Apple account, you can use the ITMS to purchase AAC-encoded music files for $.99 each. For more information about the iTunes Music Store, visit Apple's page at *http://www.apple.com/music/store*.

Mail

Mail is the standard email application that ships with Mac OS X. If you've used Mail in earlier versions of Mac OS X, you'll quickly notice a few changes to Mail's look and feel. For one, Mail no longer sports a drawer for holding your mailboxes and folders; instead, this has been incorporated into the left side of Mail's window, similar to the Finder's Sidebar. Also new with Mail are Smart Folders, which you can use to help sort and sift your email for you, similar to having your own Cliff Claven inside your computer. What's more, Spotlight indexes all your email messages, which means all your messages are searchable.

Preview

Preview lets you open (and export) files that have been saved in a variety of image formats, including PICT, GIF, JPEG, and TIFF, to name a few, and can be used to view raw PostScript files. It can also be used to open, view, and search through PDF files.

QuickTime Player

This is used for playing QuickTime movies as well as for listening to QuickTime streaming audio and video. New for Tiger, QuickTime Player supports the H.264 encoding scheme, which allows video to seamlessly scale from high-definition quality down to video you can watch on your cell phone.

Safari

Safari is a fast, Cocoa-based web browser, built by Apple specifically for Mac OS X. It is the default web browser that ships with OS X; if you want to use some other browser as the default, you can change this in Safari's preferences (Safari → Preferences → General → Default Web Browser).

New for Tiger, Safari has a built-in RSS feature. If you go to a web site that offers an RSS feed, you'll see a blue RSS icon in the address bar; click this icon to see a list of all the articles the site's feed has to offer.

Sherlock

Sherlock is Apple's venture into web services. (As mentioned earlier, the search functionality has been built into the Finder, and indexing for drives, partitions, and folders is done via the Get Info window.) To use Sherlock, you must have a connection to the Internet. Sherlock can be used to conduct searches on the Internet for:

- Pictures
- Stock quotes
- Movie theaters and show times
- The location of a business in your area (based on the address information you provide in Sherlock's preferences), as well as driving directions and a map to that location
- Bids on eBay auction items
- The arrival and departure times of airline flights
- The definition or spelling for a word in the dictionary
- Information within AppleCare's Knowledge Base to solve a problem you're having with your computer
- A quick translation from one language to another

Stickies

Stickies is a simple application that lets you create sticky notes on your screen. Similar to the notes you stick to your desk or computer, Stickies can be used to store important notes and reminders.

System Preferences

The System Preferences application is described extensively in Part IV and is addressed throughout this book.

TextEdit

TextEdit, the default application for creating text and rich text documents, also received a bit of an upgrade for Tiger. TextEdit now sports a ruler bar with text-formatting buttons for changing the alignment, leading, and indentation of text. By default, TextEdit documents are saved in rich text format (*.rtf* and *.rtfd*), but you can also save documents as plain text (*.txt*) via the Format → Make Plain Text menu option. TextEdit replaces the SimpleText application from earlier versions of the Mac OS.

Best of all, TextEdit can open Word files (*.doc*), making it possible for you to read, print, and edit files created with Microsoft Word even if you don't have Microsoft Office installed on your Mac. However, TextEdit's compatibility with Word is limited; for example, TextEdit can't interpret Word files that use change tracking.

The very last item you'll see in the Applications folder is the Utilities folder, which leads us to the next section.

Utilities

The tools found in the Utilities folder can be used to help you manage your Mac:

Activity Monitor
> The Activity Monitor lets you view the processes running on your system and provides a way for you to see the CPU load, to see how memory is allocated, and to see disk activity, disk usage, and network activity. If you click on a process name, you can see additional information about that process, or you can cancel (*kill*, in Unix-speak) by highlighting a process and choosing Process → Quit (Option-⌘-Q).

AirPort Admin Utility
> This utility is used to administer AirPort Base Stations.

AirPort Setup Assistant
> This utility is used to configure your system to connect to an AirPort wireless network.

Audio MIDI Setup
> This utility is used to add, set up, and configure Musical Instrument Digital Interface (MIDI) devices connected to your Mac. If you use GarageBand, you'll find the Audio MIDI Setup utility to be quite helpful in connecting your keyboard, guitar, or other musical device to your Mac.

Bluetooth File Exchange
> This utility allows you to exchange files with other Bluetooth-enabled devices, such as cellular phones, PDAs, and other computers. To exchange a file, launch this utility and then drag a file from the Finder to the Bluetooth File Exchange icon in the Dock. A window will appear asking you to select a recipient (or recipients) for the file.

ColorSync Utility

This utility has four main functions. By pressing the Profile First Aid icon, you can use it to verify and repair your ColorSync settings. The Profiles icon keeps track of the ColorSync profiles for your system, and the Devices icon lets you see which ColorSync devices are connected as well as the name and location of the current profile. The Filters icon lets you apply filters to selected items within a PDF document.

Console

The Console is primarily used to log the interactions between applications on your system and between those applications and the operating system itself. The Console gives you quick and easy access to system and crash logs via the Logs icon in its toolbar. The crash log created by the Console application can be used by developers to help debug their applications and should be supplied to Apple if you come across a bug in Mac OS X.

DigitalColor Meter

This small application lets you view and copy the color settings of any pixel on your screen.

Directory Access

This utility controls access for Mac OS X systems to Directory Services such as NetInfo, LDAP, Active Directory, and BSD flat files, as well as Discovery Services such as AppleTalk, Bonjour, SLP, and SMB.

Disk Utility

This utility lets you create disk images (*.dmg*) for batching and sending files (including folders and applications) from one Mac user to another. It can also be used to repair a damaged hard drive, erase rewriteable media such as CD-RWs, and initialize and partition new drives.

Grab

This utility can be used to take screenshots of your system. Two of its most useful features include the ability to select the pointer (or no pointer at all) to be displayed in the screenshot and the ability to start a 10-second timer before the screenshot is taken in order to give you the necessary time to set up the shot.

Grapher

Tiger brings back the old Apple Graphing Calculator in the form of the new Grapher utility. Use this application to plot complex math equations.

Installer

This program launches whenever you install an application on your system.

Java

The following utilities can be found in the Java directory:

Input Method Hotkey

This utility allows you to set a hot key that, when pressed while running a Java application, displays a pop-up menu that lets you select an input method.

Java Plugin Settings

This controls Java settings when Java runs in a browser. Tiger ships with two versions of this utility, one for Java 1.3.1 and another for Java 1.4.2.

Java Web Start

Java Web Start (JWS) can be used to download and run Java applications.

Keychain Access

This utility can be used to create and manage your passwords for accessing secure web and FTP sites, networked filesystems, and other items such as password-encoded files. You can also use Keychain Access to create secure, encrypted notes that can be read only by using this utility.

Migration Assistant

This utility helps you move your data from an existing Mac or Windows computer to your Mac OS X System.

NetInfo Manager

The NetInfo Manager is a tool mainly used by system and network administrators to view and edit the settings for a system. You need to have administrator privileges to use NetInfo Manager.

Network Utility

This utility is a graphical frontend to a standard set of Unix tools such as *netstat*, *ping*, *lookup*, *traceroute*, *whois*, and *finger*. It also lets you view specific information about your network connection, view stats about your AppleTalk connections, and scan the available ports for a particular domain or IP address.

ODBC Administrator

This tool allows you to connect to and exchange data with ODBC-compliant data sources. ODBC, which stands for Open Database Connectivity, is a standard database protocol supported by most database systems such as FileMaker Pro, Oracle, MySQL, and PostgreSQL. You can use ODBC Administrator to add data sources, install new database drivers, trace calls to the ODBC API, and configure connection pooling.

Printer Setup Utility

This is used to configure and control the printers connected to your computer either locally or on a network via AppleTalk, Open Directory, IP Printing, Bonjour,

USB, or Windows printing. You can also configure printers from the Print & Fax preference panel (System Preferences → Print & Fax → Printing → Set Up Printers).

NOTE

For users who are coming over from Mac OS 9, the Printer
Setup Utility replaces the Chooser for managing printers.

System Profiler

This tool (formerly known as the Apple System Profiler)
keeps track of the finer details about your system. Here,
you can view information about your particular computer; the devices (e.g., Zip or Jaz drive, CD-ROM
drives, etc.) and volumes (i.e., hard drives and partitions) connected to your Mac; and the frameworks,
extensions, and applications on your Mac.

Terminal

The Terminal application is the command-line interface
(CLI) to Mac OS X's Unix core. See "Configuring and
Using the Terminal" in Part VI for more information on
using the Terminal.

NOTE

If you really want to learn more about Unix, one book you
might want to pick up is *Learning Unix for Mac OS X Tiger*
(O'Reilly, 2005). This book teaches you the basics of Unix
and how to get the most from it on your Mac OS X system.

VoiceOver Utility

Tiger's new VoiceOver Utility provides you with an
accessible interface for your Mac—allowing you to control your Mac with your keyboard instead of with a
mouse—and provides screen-reader services for applications like Mail, Safari, and iChat, by which the computer
speaks back messages, web pages, and chat sessions.

VoiceOver is very powerful and, best of all, it's built right into the system.

X11

This is Apple's Mac OS X–compatible distribution of the X Window System. Since X11 is used primarily by long-time Unix users, it isn't installed by default, but it *is* available as one of the Custom options during the install.

Xcode Tools

Apple has gone to great lengths to lure a new breed of developers to the Mac, offering environments for traditional C, C++, Objective-C (and recently Objective-C++), Java, Perl, Python, and Ruby. With the introduction of AppleScript Studio, AppleScripters can now harness their scripting knowledge in order to build Cocoa-based applications.

Installing the Xcode Tools

You can quickly check to see whether you have the Xcode Tools installed. If you have a */Developer* directory on your hard drive, you are ready to go. If not, you'll need to install the tools either by double-clicking the *Developer.mpkg* file on Tiger's installation DVD or by downloading a disk image from the Apple Developer Connection site.

Overview of the Xcode Tools

The Xcode Tools are installed in the */Developer/Applications* directory, and additional tools are placed within the */Developer/Applications/Utilities* directory. This section briefly describes the more commonly used tools:

Interface Builder

Interface Builder is a GUI editor for both Cocoa and Carbon applications. It has complete online help and release notes you can access by launching Project Builder and using the Help menu.

Xcode

Formerly known as Project Builder, Xcode is an integrated development environment for Mac OS X. It supports both Cocoa and Carbon, using C, C++, Objective-C, and Java. Xcode also provides an interface for accessing Apple's reference documentation for the Carbon and Cocoa APIs, and it features enhancements such as code completion and distributed builds via Bonjour.

FileMerge

FileMerge compares two files or directories and lets you merge them.

PackageMaker

PackageMaker lets you package your software so that the Mac OS X Installer can install it on a user's machine.

icns Browser

The icns Browser is used to display the contents of an icon (*.icns*) file.

Icon Composer

Icon Composer is used to create *.icns* files from existing images.

Property List Editor

The Property List Editor lets you edit and create XML property lists.

For additional information about other development tools, including command-line and Java tools, see */Developer/Documentation/DeveloperTools/Tools.html*.

PART VI

Unix Basics

This part of the book is a basic introduction to show new users the Unix side of Mac OS X. Specifically, it covers:

- Configuring and using the Terminal
- Command-line editing with bash
- Additional shell commands, such as *defaults* and *open*
- Basic Unix commands

You don't have to venture into the command line if you don't want to, but it's easy to be seduced by Unix's power. Here you'll get a glimpse of what's possible with just a few easy keystrokes.

Configuring and Using the Terminal

The Terminal application (*/Applications/Utilities*) is your interface to Mac OS X's Unix shell. The Terminal can be used for everything from creating new directories (folders) and files to launching applications, and from managing and monitoring your system to programming and tweaking your system preferences.

Terminal Settings

This section offers advice on how to configure the settings for your Terminal. To open the Terminal's preference window, you'll need to use File → Show Info and change the settings from the Terminal Inspector window via the pull-down menu at the top of the window.

Change the style of the cursor?
> Display & Cursor Style → (Block, Underline, Vertical Bar).

Stop the cursor from blinking?
> Display → Cursor Style → uncheck the box next to Blink.

Change the background color and font colors of the Terminal window?
> Color → click on the color selection boxes next to Cursor, Normal Text, Selection, and Bold Text to change the color of the cursor and text in the Terminal window. When you click on a color box, another window opens with a color wheel, which allows you to select a different color. To change the background color of the Terminal window, click on the color box next to "Use this background color" in the Background Settings section.

Assign a different title to the Terminal window?
> Window → Title.

Assign a different title to the current Terminal window?
> With an open Terminal window, select File → Set Title (Shift-⌘-T). The Terminal Inspector window opens with Window selected in the pull-down menu. Enter a new title for the window in the Title field, and hit Return or Tab to change the title of the current window.

Specify the number of lines a Terminal window can contain in the scrollback buffer?
> Buffer → Buffer Size. You can either specify a number of lines in the field provided (10,000 lines is the default) or select between an unlimited scrollback or no scrollback at all.

Set the Terminal's emulation mode to VT100?
> Emulation → Strict VT-100 keypad behavior.

Close the Terminal window after I've exited?
Shell → "When the shell exits" → select either "Close the window" or "Close only if the shell exited cleanly."

Where is the history file for the shell?
It's located in your Home directory as *.bash_history*. The history file keeps track of recently entered commands, which you can recall in a variety of ways, the easiest of which is to use the Up or Down Arrows to go back or forward in the history file, respectively.

Where is bash's configuration file located?
In */private/etc/profile*.

Keyboard Shortcuts

Table 9 lists the keyboard shortcuts that can be used with the Terminal application.

Table 9. Keyboard shortcuts for use with Terminal

Key command	Description
⌘-. (period)	Terminates an active process (same as Control-C, the Unix interrupt command).
⌘–Up Arrow	Scrolls up one line at a time.
⌘–Down Arrow	Scrolls down one line at a time.
⌘–Left Arrow	Switches to previous Terminal window.
⌘–Right Arrow	Switches to next Terminal window.
⌘–Page Up[a]	Scrolls up one screen at a time.
⌘–Page Down[a]	Scrolls down one screen at a time.
⌘-Home[a]	Scrolls backward to the top of the screen.
⌘-End[a]	Scrolls forward to the bottom of the screen.
⌘-A	Selects all the text in the Terminal window, including the scrollback.
Shift-⌘-C	Opens or closes the Colors window.
⌘-I	Opens the Terminal Inspector, which allows you to change some of the Terminal's settings.

Table 9. Keyboard shortcuts for use with Terminal (continued)

Key command	Description
⌘-K	Clears all the information from the Terminal window, disabling scrollback (this is different and more extensive than the *clear* command, described later in this section).
⌘-N	Opens a new Terminal window.
Shift-⌘-N	Runs a command in a new Terminal window.
Shift-⌘-K	Makes a connection to a remote server via SSH, SFTP, FTP, or Telnet.
⌘-S	Saves the settings of the Terminal window as a *.term* file.
Shift-⌘-S	Saves the settings of the Terminal window as a differently named *.term* file.
Option-⌘-S	Saves the contents of the Terminal window, including any scrollback, as a text file.
Shift-Option-⌘-S	Saves any selected text in the Terminal window as a text file.
⌘-T	Opens the Font panel so you can change the Terminal's default font settings, including the font family, size, and color
⌘-*number*	Switches to a different Terminal window based on its *number*.

[a] Since iBooks and PowerBooks don't have a full keyboard with the Page Up, Page Down, Home, and End keys, substitute the function key (fn) for the Command key (⌘) and use the Up, Down, Left, and Right Arrow keys, respectively, to invoke these functions.

If you're security conscious (aren't we all these days?), you might want to consider enabling the Secure Keyboard Entry option, located in the Terminal's File menu. When you enable this feature, it keeps other applications (either on your Mac or over a network) from picking up the commands (and passwords) you type into the Terminal. Even if you're using SSH to make a network connection, it never hurts to have a little more security on your side to protect your passwords—and your precious data.

Additional Terminal Shortcuts

As was just illustrated, the Terminal offers dozens of special keyboard shortcuts to make your life easy, but there are a few more you can use with the *bash* shell, which are listed in Table 10.

Table 10. Additional keyboard shortcuts for use with the bash shell

Key command	Description
Control-C	Interrupts the process; cancels the previous command (⌘-. works as well).
Control-D	Used to signal end of input; terminates most programs and returns you to the shell prompt. If you issue the Control-D shortcut at a shell prompt (i.e., without a process running), the keystroke closes the Terminal window.
Control-L	Clears the display of the Terminal window (same as typing *clear* and hitting Return).
Esc-Esc	If only a partial path or filename is entered, pressing the Esc key twice completes the name of a file or file path you're attempting to enter. (Pressing the Esc key twice is the same as pressing the Tab key once.)
Tab	Has the same effect as pressing the Esc key twice.

Basic Unix Commands

If you've never used Unix before, this section serves as a quick introduction to issuing Unix commands from the Terminal. Experienced Unix users can skip over this section. For each of the following, you'll need to be using the Terminal application. The commands you need to type are shown in bold.

View a command's description and its options?

All the Unix commands on your system have a manual page (or *manpage* for short). To view the manpage for any command, you use the *man* command:

    [MacTiger:~] chuck$ **man pwd**

The instructions for using the *pwd* command (described next) are then displayed one screen at a time. If there is more than one screen for a command's description, you'll see a percentage at the lower-left corner of the Terminal window telling you how much of the manpage has been displayed. To scroll to the next screen, hit the spacebar; you'll be returned to the command prompt when you've reached the end of the manpage. Even the *man* command has its own manpage, which can be viewed by using:

```
[MacTiger:~] chuck$ man man
```

Where am I?

Type *pwd* on the command line and hit Return; this tells you the present working directory:

```
[MacTiger:~] chuck$ pwd
/Users/chuck
[MacTiger:~] chuck$
```

Change directories?

Use the *cd* command. For example, to go to the directory */Applications/Utilities*:

```
[MacTiger:~] chuck$ cd /Applications/Utilities
[MacTiger:/Applications/Utilities] chuck$
```

Go back a directory?

Use the *cd* command followed by a space and then two dots:

```
[MacTiger:/Applications/Utilities] chuck$ cd ..
[MacTiger:/Applications] chuck$
```

Return to where you were before the last cd command?

Use the *cd* command, followed by a hyphen:

```
[MacTiger:/Applications] chuck$ cd -
[MacTiger:/Applications/Utilities] chuck$
```

Go back one or more directories?

Use the *cd* command with two dots as above plus a slash and two dots (/..) for each additional directory you want to go back. For example, to go back two directories:

```
[MacTiger:/Applications/Utilities] chuck$ cd ../..
[MacTiger:/] chuck$
```

List a directory's contents?

This is accomplished using the *ls* command (see Figure 37).

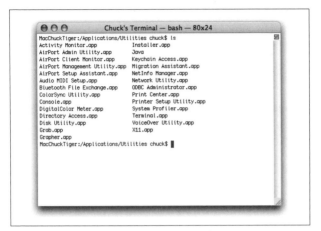

Figure 37. Listing a directory's contents with ls

By itself, the *ls* command creates a horizontal list of a directory's contents. Add the *-l* option to create a vertical list of a directory's contents, which also reveals more details about the file, directory, or application (see Figure 38).

To list all the contents for a directory, including the dot files (described in Part III), add the *-a* option (either with or without the *l* option) (see Figure 39).

When you issue a command like *ls -la*, the contents of some directories scroll up and you won't be able to see everything. One solution to this is just to issue the command and then use the Terminal window's scrollbar to go back up. Or, more efficiently, pipe (|) the command to *more*, which displays the contents of the directory one screen at a time (see Figure 40). To go to the next screen, hit the spacebar; continue doing so until you find the item for which you're looking or until you reach the end.

Get a listing of a directory's contents without seeing permissions? Use *ls -l* and pipe the output of that listing to the *colrm* (column remove) command, as follows:

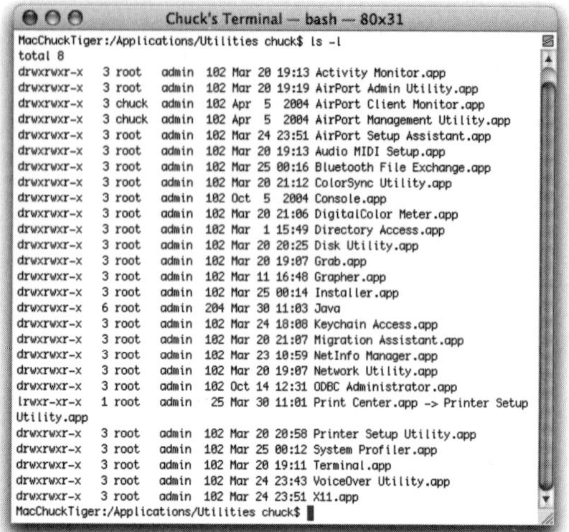

Figure 38. Listing a directory's contents with ls -l

```
[MacTiger:/Applications] chuck$ ls -l | colrm 1 48
Address Book.app
Adobe Photoshop 7
AppleScript
Automator.app
Calculator.app
Chess.app
DVD Player.app
Dashboard.app
Dictionary.app
Font Book.app
Image Capture.app
Internet Connect.app
Mail.app
Microsoft AutoUpdate.app
Microsoft Office 2004
Preview.app
QuickTime Player.app
Safari.app
Sherlock.app
Stickies.app
StuffIt Standard 9.0
```

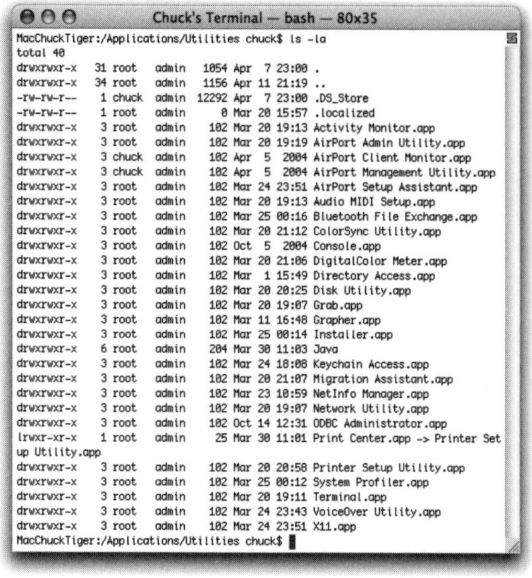

Figure 39. Listing a directory's contents, including dot files, with ls -la

```
System Preferences.app
Tablet.localized
TextEdit.app
TextWrangler.app
Utilities
iCal.app
iChat.app
iSync.app
iTunes.app
```

The numbers following *colrm* (1 and 48) are used by the command to specify a range of columns to remove. (A column in the Unix world is a single character. In this example, the column range of 1 through 48—all the characters preceding the file or directory name—are deleted.)

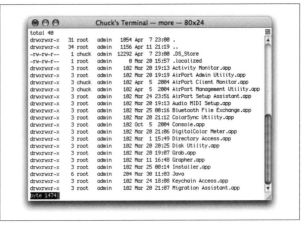

```
total 40
drwxrwxr-x  31 root   admin    1054 Apr  7 23:00 .
drwxrwxr-x  34 root   admin    1156 Apr 11 21:19 ..
-rw-rw-r--   1 chuck  admin   12292 Apr  7 23:00 .DS_Store
-rw-rw-r--   1 chuck  admin       0 Mar 20 15:57 .localized
drwxrwxr-x   3 root   admin     102 Mar 20 19:13 Activity Monitor.app
drwxrwxr-x   3 root   admin     102 Mar 20 19:19 AirPort Admin Utility.app
drwxrwxr-x   3 chuck  admin     102 Apr  5 2004 AirPort Client Monitor.app
drwxrwxr-x   3 chuck  admin     102 Apr  5 2004 AirPort Management Utility.app
drwxrwxr-x   3 root   admin     102 Mar 24 23:51 AirPort Setup Assistant.app
drwxrwxr-x   3 root   admin     102 Mar 20 19:13 Audio MIDI Setup.app
drwxrwxr-x   3 root   admin     102 Mar 25 00:16 Bluetooth File Exchange.app
drwxrwxr-x   3 root   admin     102 Mar 20 21:12 ColorSync Utility.app
drwxrwxr-x   3 root   admin     102 Oct  5 2004 Console.app
drwxrwxr-x   3 root   admin     102 Mar 20 21:06 DigitalColor Meter.app
drwxrwxr-x   3 root   admin     102 Mar  1 15:49 Directory Access.app
drwxrwxr-x   3 root   admin     102 Mar 20 20:25 Disk Utility.app
drwxrwxr-x   3 root   admin     102 Mar 20 19:07 Grab.app
drwxrwxr-x   3 root   admin     102 Mar 11 16:48 Grapher.app
drwxrwxr-x   3 root   admin     102 Mar 25 00:14 Installer.app
drwxrwxr-x   6 root   admin     204 Mar 30 11:03 Java
drwxrwxr-x   3 root   admin     102 Mar 24 18:08 Keychain Access.app
drwxrwxr-x   3 root   admin     102 Mar 20 21:07 Migration Assistant.app
byte 1474
```

Figure 40. Listing a directory's contents with some assistance from the more command

Clear the display?

When you issue the *clear* command, the Terminal window scrolls down, placing the command prompt at the top of the display:

```
[MacTiger:/Applications] chuck$ clear
```

You can also use Control-L to clear the display; if you want to reset the Terminal window, use ⌘-K to clear the window's scrollback.

Create a new directory (folder)?

Use the *mkdir* command followed by the name of the new directory you'd like to create:

```
[MacTiger:~] chuck$ mkdir NewDirectory
```

Remove an empty directory?

Use the *rmdir* command:

```
[MacTiger:~] chuck$ rmdir NewDirectory
```

Remove a directory and all its contents, including subdirectories?

Use the *rm* command with the *-rf* option to force the removal of the directory and its contents:

```
[MacTiger:~] chuck$ rm -rf NewDirectory
```

Create an empty file?

There are many ways you can do this, but one of the easiest is by using the *touch* command:

```
[MacTiger:~] chuck$ touch myfile.txt
```

Copy a file or directory?

Use the *cp* command:

```
[MacTiger:~] chuck$ cp myfile.txt myfile2.txt
```

This makes a copy of *myfile.txt* named *myfile2.txt* within the same directory. If you want to copy a file and place it in another directory, use the following:

```
[MacTiger:~] chuck$ cp myfile.txt Books/myfile.txt
```

This makes a copy of *myfile.txt* and places that copy in the *Books* directory.

Rename a file or directory?

To rename a file, use the *mv* command:

```
[MacTiger:~] chuck$ mv myfile.txt myFile.txt
```

This renames the file *myfile.txt* to *myFile.txt* in the same directory.

Move a file or directory?

The following moves the file *myFile.txt* to the *Books* directory:

```
[MacTiger:~] chuck$ mv myFile.txt Books
```

See what's inside a file?

For this, you can use either *cat*, *more*, or *less*:

```
[MacTiger:~/Books] chuck$ cat myFile.txt
This is my file. I hope you like it.
Chuck
[MacTiger:~/Books] chuck$
```

Make a file or directory read-only?

For this, you'll need to use the *chmod* (change mode) command. Any one of the following will assign read-only permission to *myFile.txt* for everyone:

```
[MacTiger:~/Books] chuck$ chmod =r myFile.txt
[MacTiger:~/Books] chuck$ chmod 444 myFile.txt
[MacTiger:~/Books] chuck$ chmod a-wx,a+r myFile.txt
```

The *chmod* command has many options; for more information, see its manpage (*man chmod*).

Zip up a file so I can send it to a Windows user?

To zip a file or directory, use the *zip* command, as follows:

```
[MacTiger:~/Books] chuck$ zip myFile.zip myFile.txt
```

This zips up the file and places the *myFile.zip* file in the same directory as the original file.

View the contents of a Zip file?

Use the *unzip* command with the *-l* option to list the contents of a Zip file, as follows:

```
[MacTiger:~/Books] chuck$ unzip -l myFile.zip
Archive:  myFile.zip
  Length     Date    Time    Name
  ------     ----    ----    ----
       0   09-18-102  20:20   myFile.txt
  ------                     -------
       0                     1 file
```

This shows that there is one file in *myFile.zip* (*myFile.txt*). It also shows the size of the file (in kilobytes) and the date and time that the file was created.

Unzip a file that I received from a Windows user?

To unzip a file or directory, use the *unzip* command, as follows:

```
[MacTiger:~/Books] chuck$ unzip myFile.zip
```

This unzips the file and places its contents in the current directory. If a file with the same name is already in that directory, Unix asks you what you want to do:

```
[MacTiger:~/Books] chuck$ unzip myFile.zip
Archive:  myFile.zip
```

```
replace myFile.txt? [y]es, [n]o, [A]ll, [N]one,
[r]ename: r
new name: myFile.txt.bak
extracting: myFile2.txt
```

You are given the following options to replace the existing file(s):

y

> For yes

n

> For no

A

> To replace all the files with similar names

N

> To replace none of the files

r

> To rename the like-named file that already exists. If you choose to rename the existing file (as shown in this example), you are prompted to enter a new name for that file; doing so changes that file's name. The *unzip* command then extracts the Zip file.

Archive a file or directory?

To archive (and compress) a file or directory, use the Unix tape archive command, *tar*, as follows:

```
[MacTiger:~/Books] chuck$ tar cvfz myFile.tar.gz ↵
myFile.txt
```

The options used are as follows:

c

> Creates a new archive

v

> Verbose; prints the filenames onscreen as files that are added to or extracted from the archive

f

> Stores files in, or extracts files from, an archive

---

z
: Uses *gzip* to zip, or compress, the archive

View the contents of a tar archive?

To peek inside a *.tar.gz* or *.tgz* file in order to see what it contains, use the *tar* command with the *tvfz* options:

```
[MacTiger:~/Books] chuck$ tar tvfz myFile.tar.gz
-rw-r--r--  1 chuck  staff  44 Oct 05 21:10 myFile.txt
```

The *t* option is used to print the names of the files inside the tarball.

Open a .tar file?

To unpack a tarball (a *.tar* file), use the following:

```
[MacTiger:~/Books] chuck$ tar xvf myFile.tar myFile.txt
```

The *x* option is used to extract the contents of the tarball. This command unpacks the tarball and places its contents in the file *myFile.txt*.

If you receive a *.tgz* (or *.tar.gz*) file, it means the tarball has been compressed using *gzip*. To decompress that file, use the following command:

```
[MacTiger:~/Books] chuck$ tar xvfz myFile.tgz myFile.txt
```

The *z* option tells the *tar* command that the file it will decompress has been *gzip*'d.

Log in as the superuser?

Some commands require you to be the superuser (or the *root* user) before they can be issued. Rather than logging out and then logging back in as *root*, you can issue the *su* command, which will then be prompt you to type the superuser's password:

```
[MacTiger:~] chuck$ su
Password: ********
[MacTiger:/Users/chuck] root#
```

Now you have ultimate power; use it with great care, because you could damage or overwrite something vital. When you are finished, issue the *exit* command to go back to being a normal user:

```
[MacTiger:/Users/chuck] root# exit
exit
[MacTiger:~] chuck$
```

NOTE

For most (if not all) tasks, you should be able to get by with using the *sudo* command instead of logging in as *root*.

For more information about using the Unix side of Mac OS X, pick up a copy of *Learning Unix for Mac OS X Tiger* (O'Reilly, 2005). To learn more about the *bash* shell, pick up a copy of *Learning the bash Shell* (O'Reilly, 2005).

Special Mac Unix Commands

One of the first things that traditional Unix users will notice when they start poking around in the Terminal is that there are a few new commands they'll need to add to their repertoire. Two that we'll discuss in this section are *defaults* and *open*.

Finding Stuff with locate

One of the more useful Unix commands you'll use in the Terminal is the *locate* command. This aptly named command does just what its name implies—it locates files for you. But unlike Spotlight, *locate*'s searches are limited to file and folder (directory) names.

Don't get ahead of yourself, though; don't just pop open a Terminal window and type in *locate* followed by a filename and expect the command to work. The way *locate* returns its results so quickly is by sifting through what is known as the *locate database*, which is basically a big file that lists the file and folder names for everything on your Mac's hard drive. Before *locate* will work you need to create the locate database, so let's move on to that.

Creating the locate database

To create *locate*'s database, you'll first need to have a Terminal window open and at the ready. Follow this sequence to build the *locate* database:

1. At the command prompt, enter the following command:

   ```
   $ cd /usr/libexec
   ```

   This takes you to a directory that contains a little program you'll need to use to build the *locate* database.

2. The program you will be using is named *locate.updatedb*. However, if you just type *locate.updatedb* at the command line and hit Return, nothing happens. That's because only a user with administrator privileges can run this command. In order to run the program to build *locate*'s database, you'll need to use the *sudo* command, as follows:

   ```
   $ sudo ./locate.updatedb
   ```

   After you enter this command, you are prompted to enter your password. If you have administrator privileges on your Mac, just enter the password you use to log in to your account. The command works as follows: After the user correctly enters an administrator's password, the "./" (often referred to as "dot-slash" in geek-speak) tells the shell that the next bit of text is a command that needs to run when the Return key is hit (or "entered"). The *locate.updatedb* program then leaps into action, careening through your Mac's hard drive, cataloging all your file and folder names into the *locate* database.

That's it. That's all it takes to build your locate database. If you leave your Mac on overnight, and if you don't have it set to go to sleep, Unix builds your locate database for you automatically as part of a *cron* job (sort of a janitorial service Unix performs on your Mac every day around 4 a.m.). If you don't leave your Mac on overnight, you'll need to rebuild the *locate* database (using the commands in steps 1 and 2) regularly, as the *locate.updatedb* program doesn't work automatically or run in the background as does Spotlight.

Searching with locate

Now that you know what *locate* is and how to build its database, you can use it to search for files and folders on your Mac. For example, you could use the following command to locate all of the Word documents on your system:

```
$ locate *.doc
```

In this example the asterisk (*) is used as a wildcard to mean any character, so the Unix shell looks for any files that end with *.doc* (the file extension for Word documents). Or, if you can remember the filename but can't remember where you saved the file, you could use something like this:

```
$ locate mosxpg4_ch06.doc
/Users/chuck/Documents/TigerPocketGuide/mosxpg4_ch06.doc
```

This tells me that the file I'm looking for (*mosxpg4_ch06.doc*) is located in my TigerPocketGuide folder, which is inside my Documents folder.

Why Should I Use locate When I Have Spotlight?

Good question. Fortunately for you, the answer is fairly short.

The advantage of using the *locate* command is that it returns only the file and/or folder names that match your search criteria. So, if you have a file named *BigBopper.doc*, but you can't remember where you saved it, you can type in *locate BigBopper* and—if you've recently built or rebuilt the *locate* database—you'll get a quick response telling you exactly where that file is on your Mac.

However, if you were to search your Mac with Spotlight by just typing *BigBopper* into Spotlight's search field, your results would show not only that file, but a list of every other file or folder on your system containing "BigBopper" in its name or content. This means you could get a lot of false-positives in your Spotlight search results if you're searching for a common phrase.

Of course, the advantage of using Spotlight is that it not only finds the file for you, but allows you to open it by double-clicking on it in Spotlight's results.

As you can see, there are advantages to each method; deciding which to use is simply a matter of figuring out which search method (*locate* or Spotlight) will best resolve your current predicament.

Change and Set Preferences with defaults

When you customize your Mac using the System Preferences or an application's preferences, all those changes and settings are stored in what's known as the preferences system. The command-line utility to change your preferences is the *defaults* command. Everything you've done to make your Mac your own is stored as XML data in the form of a property list (or *plist*), and your property lists are stored in ~/Library/Preferences.

WARNING

The *defaults* command is not for the foolhardy. If you're uncomfortable with the command line or unsure how to change a setting properly, you should stick to using the application's Preferences pane rather than attempting to use the *defaults* command.

If you *do* manage to mangle your settings, the easiest way to correct the problem is to go back to that application's Preferences pane and reset your preferences. Another solution is to delete the preferences file for the application from ~/Library/Preferences.

Every time you change one of these settings, the corresponding property list is updated. For the initiated, there are two other ways to alter the property lists. The first is by using the Property List Editor application (*/Developer/Applications*), and the other is by using the *defaults* command in the Terminal. Extensive coverage of these is beyond the scope of this book, but here are a few basic examples of how to use the *defaults* command.

Examples

The following are some examples of how to use the *defaults* command:

View all the user defaults on your system
> `$ defaults domains`
> This prints a listing of all the domains in the user's defaults system. The items in the list are run together with spaces in between—not quite the prettiest way to view them.

View the settings for your Dock

```
$ defaults read com.apple.dock
```

This reads the settings from the *com.apple.dock.plist* file, found in *~/Library/Preferences*. This listing is rather long, so you might want to adjust the output in order to view the contents one screen at a time:

```
$ defaults read com.apple.dock | more
```

Change the location of your Dock to the top of the screen

Near the beginning of that listing, look for the following:

```
orientation = bottom;
```

You'll see that its value is set to bottom, which means your Dock is located at the bottom of the screen. To change that setting, type the following:

```
$ defaults write com.apple.dock orientation top
```

After a short pause, you're returned to another command prompt, but you'll notice that the Dock is still located at the bottom of the screen. Unlike most changes you make with the *defaults* command, changes to the Dock take effect only after you log out and log back in.

Enter *exit* to quit the Terminal. Then save any changes in other applications and quit them, too. Now log out and log back in to your system (⬤ → Log Out, or Shift-⌘-Q). When you log back in, you'll see the Dock, in all its glory, floating just below the menu bar at the top of the screen. To quickly change its location back to the bottom of the screen (or to the left or right side), use ⬤ → Dock → Position on (Left, Bottom, or Right).

For additional options and to learn more about how to use the *defaults* command, enter *defaults –help* or view the defaults manpage (*man defaults*).

Using the open Command

With Mac OS X, you can launch any application from the command line using the *open* command. There are three ways to invoke this command:

---

open filename

> This opens the file and its associated application if they aren't already running. For example:
>
> ```
> $ open textFile.txt
> ```
>
> opens the file *textFile.txt* using the default text editor, which is TextEdit.

open -a application_path filename

> The *-a* option lets you specify the application to use when opening the file. For example, to open the *textFile.txt* file in BBEdit (*http://www.barebones.com*) instead of TextEdit, you need to do the following:
>
> ```
> $ open -a BBEdit textFile.txt
> ```
>
> While that might look odd, the command springs into action by launching BBEdit and opening the *textFile.txt* file in one fell swoop.

open -e filename_path

> The *-e* option forces the use of the TextEdit application. For example:
>
> ```
> $ open -e ~/Books/Templates/proposal_template.txt
> ```

Here are some additional examples of how to use the Terminal to open files and launch applications:

Open an HTML page using a browser other than Safari?

> The way to do this is to specify the application, using the *-a* option:
>
> ```
> $ open -a Firefox ~/Sites/index.html
> ```
>
> The *-a* option is used in this case to launch Firefox (*http://www.mozilla.org/products/firefox*), which, if you have it installed on your system, is located in your Sites folder.

Launch Classic from the Terminal?

> If you find yourself using the Classic environment, one way you can launch Classic from the Terminal is by typing the following:
>
> ```
> $ open /System/Library/CoreServices/Classic Startup.app
> ```

Though that does the trick, a faster way to do the same thing is to set up an alias in the shell. To do this, enter the following on the command line:

```
$ alias classic='open -a ⏎
/System/Library/CoreServices/Classic Startup.app'
```

Spotlight's Metadata Utilities

When Apple added Spotlight to Mac OS X Tiger, it didn't stop with providing graphical tools for searching, but also built a number of Unix command-line utilities for using Spotlight from the Terminal. Here they are:

mdfind

Used to search through Spotlight's metadata store and return a list of results that match your search criteria. For example, if you wanted to find out where the clownfish desktop image is saved on your computer, you could use the following:

```
$ mdfind clown
/Library/Desktop Pictures/Nature/Clown Fish.jpg
```

mdimport

Used to import metadata from a file, folder, or disk. For example, if you wanted Spotlight to import metadata for the files in a project folder a coworker sent you, you would use the following:

```
$ mdimport ~/Documents/NewBooks/
```

mdls

Used to list the metadata for a file. For example, here's all the metadata Spotlight has collected for the file containing this part of the book:

```
$ mdls mosxpg4_ch06.doc
mosxpg4_ch06.doc -------------
kMDItemAttributeChangeDate     = 2005-04-13 03:26:15 -
0700
kMDItemAuthors                 = ("Chuck Toporek")
kMDItemContentCreationDate     = 2005-03-30 07:41:19 -
0800
```

```
kMDItemContentModificationDate = 2005-04-13 03:26:14 -
0700
kMDItemContentType              = "com.microsoft.word.
doc"
kMDItemContentTypeTree          = (
    "com.microsoft.word.doc",
    "public.data",
    "public.item",
    "public.composite-content",
    "public.content"
)
kMDItemDisplayName              = "mosxpg4_ch06.doc"
kMDItemFSContentChangeDate       = 2005-04-13 03:26:14 -
0700
kMDItemFSCreationDate            = 2005-03-30 07:41:19 -
0800
kMDItemFSCreatorCode             = 1297307460
kMDItemFSFinderFlags             = 0
kMDItemFSInvisible               = 0
kMDItemFSLabel                   = 0
kMDItemFSName                    = "mosxpg4_ch06.doc"
kMDItemFSNodeCount               = 0
kMDItemFSOwnerGroupID            = 501
kMDItemFSOwnerUserID             = 501
kMDItemFSSize                    = 269636
kMDItemFSTypeCode                = 1463304782
kMDItemID                        = 213422
kMDItemKind                      = "Microsoft Word
document"
kMDItemLastUsedDate              = 2005-04-13 02:20:44 -
0700
kMDItemTitle                     = "6"
kMDItemUsedDates                 = (
    2005-04-05 21:27:03 -0700,
    2005-04-05 17:00:00 -0700,
    2005-04-12 17:00:00 -0700
)
```

On the left, you'll see a bunch of lines of text starting
with kMD; these are metadata keys, which you can use
with the *mdfind* command. For example, if you wanted
to find all the files that changed on a certain date, you
could use the following:

```
$ mdfind "kMDItemAttributeChangeDate" == "2005-04-13"
/Users/chuck/Documents/mosxpg4_forprod/mosxpg4_ch06.doc
```

This comes in handy when you're writing a backup script and you want to find the files that have changed on a given day.

There are other Spotlight-related Unix commands, but these three will prove to be the most useful for most users. If you want to find out more information about these commands, read their manpages (*man mdfind*, *man mdimport*, or *man mdls*); if you're interested in other metadata commands, you can find them in */usr/bin*.

The root User Account

On any Unix system, the *root* user account has the authority to issue any command, giving anyone using it extreme power. Because of the risks associated with this power (such as the ability to permanently delete the entire filesystem), the *root* user account is disabled by default on Mac OS X. However, there are two ways you can enable it: by using NetInfo Manager or by using the command line. In both cases, you must already have administrator privileges on the system.

NOTE

If you're the only user on the system, you will have administrator privileges by default. As such, if there is a particular function or command that can be issued only by the *root* user, you should use the *sudo* command.

Follow these steps to enable the *root* user account from NetInfo Manager:

1. Launch NetInfo Manager (*/Applications/Utilities*).

2. To make changes to the NetInfo settings, click on the padlock in the lower-left corner of the NetInfo window. You are asked for the administrator's name and password; enter those and click OK.

3. In the menu bar, select Security → Enable Root User.

4. You are asked to enter a password for the *root* user. The *root* password must be more than five characters in length. Click OK and then enter the password again to confirm it. Click on the Verify button to confirm the password and enable the root account.

5. If you have no further changes to make in NetInfo Manager, click on the padlock at the lower-left of the window to prevent further changes from being made; then quit the application (⌘-Q).

To enable the *root* user account using the Terminal, enter the following command:

```
[MacTiger:~] chuck$ sudo passwd root
Password: *******
Changing password for root.
New password: ********
Retype new password: ********
[MacTiger:~] chuck$
```

NOTE

The asterisks shown in this example won't appear onscreen when you enter the passwords; actually, nothing happens onscreen. If you make a mistake while entering the password, you can hit the Backspace or Delete key to remove what you've typed, then simply re-enter the password.

The first time you're asked for a password, enter your own. Once the system verifies that you have administrator privileges, you're asked to enter and confirm a new password for the *root* user account. Once the *root* account has been assigned a password, you can use it to log in with the username *root*.

If you find you need to access a directory or issue a command that requires *root* (or superuser) privileges, you can temporarily log in as the *root* user by issuing the *su* command:

```
[MacTiger:~] chuck$ su
Password: ********
[MacTiger:/Users/chuck] chuck#
```

Notice how the prompt has changed from chuck$ to chuck#. The # prompt is an indicator that you are running as *root*. As *root*, you should be careful of what you type.

After you've finished your business as *root*, type *exit* and hit Return to log out as the *root* user and return to your normal user prompt.

NOTE

The *root* user's home directory can be found in */private/var/root*.

PART VII

Configuring Your Mac

You know that feeling you got when you first unpacked your Mac? You know, the anticipation you felt while you carefully opened the box, the rush of pulling all the clear plastic coverings off the power supply and untying the cables, plugging your precious Mac in, hitting the Power-On button, and finally hearing that "bwong" sound as your Mac started up? Well, that same anticipation is bound to hit you after installing Mac OS X Tiger. As you explore the system, you're certain to have lots of questions about setting things up and enabling certain checkboxes. This chapter should ease your transition and help you get your Tiger system set up just the way you want it. It presents helpful tips and tricks for configuring your Mac in a simple Q&A format. Each item starts with a simple "How do I..." question, followed by the steps you'll need to take to accomplish that task. For example:

> *Change the color depth of my display?*
> System Preferences → Displays → Display → Colors
> → select from 256 Colors, Thousands, or Millions.

Can't find something you're looking for? Flip to the back of the book and look in the Index to see if your question is covered here or elsewhere in the book. The tasks are divided into the following sections:

- Customizing the System
- Files and Folders
- Fonts and Font Management

- Spotlight and Searching for Files
- Obtaining Information About the System
- .Mac
- Safari and the Internet
- Mail.app
- Modems and Dial-Up Networking
- Networking
- AirPort and Wireless Networking
- Printer Configuration and Printing
- Maintenance and Troubleshooting

If you're new to Mac OS X, or if you just need to jog your memory because you can't quite remember the location of a particular setting, this is the place to start.

TIP

As you're configuring your Mac and switching back and forth between various System Preference panels, use ⌘-L to quickly switch back to System Preference's main window.

Customizing the System

The following are options you can use to customize the "Aqua look and feel" of your system:

Change the resolution of my display?
    System Preferences → Displays → Display → select a resolution that suits your needs.

Change my desktop image?
    System Preferences → Desktop & Screen Saver → Desktop.

    Control-click on the desktop itself and select Change Desktop Background from the context menu.

If you have iPhoto, select one of the images in your iPhoto Library and click the Desktop button at the bottom of iPhoto's window.

Have the pictures on my desktop change automatically?

System Preferences → Desktop & Screen Saver → Desktop; click the checkbox next to "Change picture" and select an interval from the pull-down menu.

Use one of the Mac OS 9 background images for my desktop instead of the (boring) ones that come with Mac OS X?

System Preferences → Desktop & Screen Saver → Desktop → Choose Folder. A Finder sheet slides down; use this to navigate to Mac OS 9 System Folder → Appearance → Desktop Pictures. Then select one of the following folders and click the Choose button: 3D Graphics, Convergency, Ensemble Photos, or Photos. The images in the directory you choose become part of your Desktop Collection.

Add a new background pattern and make it available to all users?

Create or save the image to either the Abstract, Nature, or Solid Colors folder in */Library/Desktop Pictures*.

Change the double-click speed of my mouse?

System Preferences → Keyboard & Mouse → Mouse or Trackpad panel.

Change the scrolling speed of my scrollwheel mouse?

System Preferences → Keyboard & Mouse → Mouse panel → Scrolling Speed.

Change the settings on my iBook's trackpad to make it emulate mouse clicks?

System Preferences → Keyboard & Mouse → Trackpad panel → Trackpad Gestures → select the checkboxes for the items you want. The items include Clicking, Dragging, and Drag Lock (tap again to release).

Disable my PowerBook's trackpad when I'm using a Bluetooth mouse?

System Preferences → Keyboard & Mouse → Trackpad panel → Trackpad Options → select the checkbox for "Ignore trackpad when mouse is present."

Change the password for my user account?

System Preferences → Accounts → click on your username → Password → Change Password.

Use Tiger's new Password Assistant to help me choose a secure password?

System Preferences → Accounts → click on your username → Password → Change Password → enter your Old Password → click the "key" icon to the right of the New Password field. Clicking this pops open the Password Assistant shown in Figure 41. Select the Type of password you want to use and then move the Length slider right or left to get a longer or shorter password, respectively. When you've found a password you're comfortable with, jot it down somewhere and then close the window; the password is applied to your account.

Change the date/time?

System Preferences → Date & Time → Date & Time panel.

Specify how the date and time appear in the menu bar?

System Preferences → Date & Time → Clock → Show the date and time.

Specify the date and time settings for another country while I'm traveling?

To change the date: System Preferences → International → Formats → select a country from the Region pull-down menu.

To change the time: System Preferences → International → Formats → select a country from the Region pull-down menu.

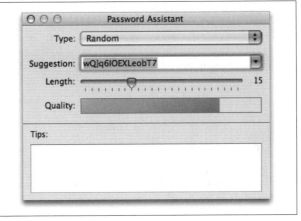

Figure 41. Tiger's new Password Assistant helps you keep your Mac secure by finding you a hard-to-guess password.

Set up my Mac to tell me what time it is?

System Preferences → Date & Time → Clock → click the checkbox next to "Announce the time" → select how frequently you'd like your Mac to announce the time from the pop-up menu.

Use a network time server to set my clock's time?

System Preferences → Date & Time → Date & Time; click on the checkbox next to "Set date & time automatically" → select an NTP Server in the scroll list.

NOTE

You must be connected to the Internet to use a network time server. One helpful hint is to use the network time server to set an accurate time for your system, then uncheck the "Set date & time automatically" box. This keeps your Mac from checking in with the server every time you restart it.

Set my time zone?

System Preferences → Date & Time → Time Zone. When you do this, a map of the world appears; simply click and drag the time-zone bar to your location on the map and let go of the mouse. As you move the time-zone bar, the date and time in the menu bar change dynamically.

Display the current date and time from the command line?

Use the *date* command:

```
MacTiger:~ chuck$ date
Mon Jun 6 20:33:43 PDT 2005
```

Find out how long my system has been running?

Use the *uptime* command:

```
[MacTiger:~] chuck$ uptime
21:50  up  10:09, 2 users, load averages: 0.30 0.55 0.
54
```

The *uptime* command displays the following in the order that they appear: the current time (21:50, or 9:50 p.m.), how long the system has been running (up 10:09, or 10 hours 9 minutes), the number of users logged into the system, and the load averages on the processor.

Change the name of my computer?

System Preferences → Sharing; enter the new name for your computer in the Computer Name text box.

Display the battery status for my PowerBook in the menu bar?

System Preferences → Energy Saver → Options pane → select the checkbox next to "Show battery status in menu bar."

Display a volume control in the menu bar?

System Preferences → Sound → select the checkbox next to "Show volume in menu bar."

Quickly open the Sound preferences panel?

Hold down the Option key and press one of the volume keys (mute, or volume up/down) on your keyboard.

For PowerBook and iBook, the volume keys are as follows:

- Mute: F3
- Volume Down: F4
- Volume Up: F5

If you have an Apple Keyboard (wireless or USB) with a number pad, the volume keys are located across the top row of the number pad, to the right.

Set up my computer to check for updates to the system automatically?

System Preferences → Software Update → Update Software → select the checkbox next to "Automatically check for updates when you have a network connection," and then select the frequency (Daily, Weekly, Monthly) from the pull-down menu.

Set up my computer to start an application automatically after I log in?

System Preferences → Accounts → click on your username → Login Items. Click the Add button (+) and then use the Finder sheet to select the application(s) you would like your Mac to start after you log in.

You can also drag an application icon from the Finder to the window in the Login Items pane within the Accounts panel.

Remove an application from my Login Items list?

System Preferences → Accounts → click on your username → Login Items → select the application name you want to remove from the list → either click the minus button (–) or press the Delete key on your keyboard.

Adjust the amount of time my system must be idle before the screen saver kicks in?

System Preferences → Desktop & Screen Saver → Screen Saver → adjust the slider next to "Start screen saver."

Quickly activate my screen saver when I know I'll be away from my desk for a while?

System Preferences → Desktop & Screen Saver → Screen Saver → click the Hot Corners button at the bottom of the window → use the pop-up menus to mark one of the corners of your screen for "Start Screen Saver." Now when you want to enable the screen saver, all you need to do is move the mouse to that corner of the screen.

Protect my system from prying eyes while I'm away from my computer?

System Preferences → Security → enable the checkbox next to "Require password to wake this computer from sleep or screen saver."

Change the background of a window to a different color or to an image?

Finder → View → as Icons, then use View → Show View Options (⌘-J); select either Color or Picture for the Background options.

NOTE

You cannot change the background of the Finder window if the View is set to "as Columns."

Set up my computer to start up or shut down at the same time every day?

System Preferences → Energy Saver → click the Schedule button.

Set up my computer to restart automatically after a power failure?

System Preferences → Energy Saver → Options → enable the checkbox next to "Restart automatically after a power failure."

Enable full keyboard access so I can navigate my system and select menu items without using a mouse?

System Preferences → Keyboard & Mouse → Keyboard Shortcuts → Full keyboard access → click the radio button for "All controls."

Use the RSS screen saver?

To change Tiger's default screen saver so that it uses the RSS feed, follow these steps:

1. Open System Preferences.

2. Click the Screen Saver tab.

3. In the list of available Screen Savers to the left, select "RSS Visualizer."

4. After selecting RSS Visualizer, you'll see a demo of the RSS screen saver in the display to the right.

By default, Tiger's RSS screen saver calls up news items from Apple's Hot News RSS feed. If you want to select a different site:

1. Click the Options button.

2. A sheet slides out, displaying a list of other "pre-ordained" RSS sites which you can choose from.

3. Select a feed (for example, the O'Reilly Network feed).

4. Click the Done button.

5. To see what the screen saver looks like, click the Test button.

Now when the screen saver jumps into action, you'll see news items fed to you from the O'Reilly Network of sites, including the Mac DevCenter.

NOTE

Your computer must have a Quartz Extreme–compatible graphics card in order that the RSS Visualizer even appear in the list. If you don't see this item in the list of available screen savers, your Mac won't be able to use this feature.

Register my license number for QuickTime Pro?

System Preferences → QuickTime → click the Registration button and enter your license number.

Set a Keyboard Shortcut for Secure Empty Trash?

If you want to add a keyboard shortcut for Secure Empty Trash, you can do so by taking the following steps:

1. Launch System Preferences by clicking its icon in the Dock.

2. Select the Keyboard & Mouse preference panel.

3. Select the Keyboard Shortcuts tab.

4. Beneath the list of keyboard shortcuts in the middle of the window, you'll see plus (+) and minus (–) sign buttons. Click the plus button to add an item to the list.

5. In the sheet that slides out of the window's titlebar, select Finder from the Application pop-up menu.

6. In the Menu Title field, type in "Secure Empty Trash." This tells the Finder to look for this menu item.

7. Tab down to the Keyboard Shortcut field and create a keyboard shortcut that works for you. For example, you could set the keyboard shortcut for Secure Empty Trash to Control-Shift-⌘-D.

8. Quit System Preferences (⌘-Q).

9. Because you've made changes to the Finder, you'll need to restart it. To do this, go to → Force Quit (Option-⌘-Esc) to open the Force Quit window.

10. Select the Finder and then click the Relaunch button. After clicking the Relaunch button, you'll be prompted with an alert dialog box asking if you really want to relaunch the Finder. Since this is what you want to do, click on the Relaunch button in the sheet. After a brief pause, your Dock quits and restarts.

11. Close the Force Quit window by clicking on the red close-window icon in the window's titlebar.

12. Now if you go to the Finder's application menu, you'll see that the keyboard shortcut you've added for Secure Empty Trash shows up in the menu. Before using this shortcut, just make sure the files in your Trash are files that you'll never, ever need again.

Files and Folders

The following are options to use with files and folders:

Create a new folder?
Control-click → New Folder (in the Finder or on the desktop).

Shift-⌘-N.

NOTE

In earlier versions of the Mac OS, ⌘-N was used to create new folders; now, ⌘-N is used for opening a new Finder window.

Rename a file or folder?
Click once on the icon and then click once on the name of the file to highlight it (or press Return). Type in the new name for the file or folder and hit Return to accept the new name.

Click on the icon, then use ⌘-I to open the Get Info window. Click on the disclosure triangle next to Name & Extension and enter the new file or directory name.

In the Terminal, use the following command:

```
MacTiger:~ chuck$ mv myFile.txt yourFile.txt
```

The *mv* command changes the name of *myFile.txt* to *yourFile.txt*.

Use Smart Folders to organize my files?

One of the things you'll notice with Tiger is that Smart Folders are everywhere—and that's a good thing. Beyond using Smart Folders to organize your music in iTunes, you can now use them to help you organize files with the Finder. For example, let's say you want to keep track of all the files you've modified today, probably as a means of backing them up once your workday is done. To create a Smart Folder to track these files, do the following:

1. Open the Finder and go to your Documents folder.

2. From the File menu, select New Smart Folder (Option-⌘-N); the Finder window changes slightly, giving you options for setting the Smart Folder's filtering criteria.

3. Beneath the Finder's toolbar you'll see a darker gray bar with buttons for Servers, Computer, Home, and Others.... By default, this is set to Computer, but since you don't want system files included, click Home so the Smart Folder looks only in your Home folder and its subfolders (such as Documents, Movies, etc.). There's also a Save button to the far right, but don't click on that just yet.

4. Leave the first row of pop ups set to Kind and Any.

5. In the second row of pop ups, change Last Opened to Last Modified, and change Any Date to Today.

6. At the end of the second row, click the + button to add a third row.

7. Change Last Opened to Created, and change Any Date to Today.

8. Now click the Save button; you'll be asked to enter a name for the folder, so give it a name like Created/Modified Today.

9. Leave the Where pop-up set to Saved Searches, and leave the Add To Sidebar checkbox checked.

10. Click the Save button.

The new Smart Folder appears in the Finder's Sidebar and gives you quick access to finding the files you created or modified today. Keep in mind that this Smart Folder's contents changes daily, so if you're planning to back up the items in this folder, you'll need to do it before midnight.

Create a Burn Folder to help me back up important files?

In the Finder, go to the location where you want to create the Burn Folder and follow these steps:

1. From the File menu, select New Burn Folder.

NOTE

There is no keyboard shortcut for creating a new Burn Folder. However, if you follow the same steps and principles for adding a keyboard shortcut for the Secure Empty Trash item, you can quickly create a New Burn Folder shortcut in the same way.

---

2. Change the name of the folder from "Burn Folder" to some other name appropriate for your needs (such as "Files2Burn").

3. Drag and drop any items (files, folders, applications, whatever) to the Burn Folder. Mac OS X places an alias of these items inside the Burn Folder.

To actually burn a CD from the Burn Folder:

1. Select the Burn Folder in the Finder. When you do this, you'll notice that a grayish-black bar appears in

the Finder's view, with a Burn button at its right edge.

2. When you click the Burn button, you'll be asked to insert a blank CD; go ahead and do so.

3. If the blank CD you've inserted is accepted by the drive, another window pops up, allowing you to assign a name to the disc you're about to burn. By default, the name is set to that of the Burn Folder (in this case, Files2Burn).

4. To burn the files to CD, click the Burn button.

NOTE

While you can drag a Smart Folder from your Saved Searches folder (*~/Library/Saved Searches*) to a Burn Folder to create an alias of it there, the files found by the Smart Folder's search criteria, unfortunately, don't get brought along. When you burn a copy of the Burn Folder, you're burning a copy of the *.savedSearch* item and not, as you may have hoped, the files found by the Smart Folder's search criteria.

Change the program associated with a particular extension?
Click on a file and then use ⌘-I or File → Get Info. Click on the disclosure triangle next to "Open with" and either select one of the applications from the pull-down menu or choose Other to select a different program. If you want to specify the application you selected as the default for opening files with that particular extension, click Change All; otherwise, close the Info window to save the changes.

Change the permissions for a file or directory?
Click on a file or directory and then use ⌘-I or File → Get Info. Click on the disclosure triangle next to Ownership & Permissions to change the access for Owner, Group, and Others.

Use the *chmod* command. To learn more about *chmod* and its options, see its manpage (*man chmod*).

Copy a file to the desktop instead of moving it or creating a shortcut?

Select the file, then Option-drag the icon to the desktop (notice that a plus sign appears next to the pointer in a green bubble) and release the mouse button.

In the Finder, select the file → Edit → Copy filename → click on the Home icon in the Finder's sidebar → double-click on the Desktop icon → Edit → Paste item.

Find out where an open document is saved on my system?

Command-click on the name of the document in the titlebar. A menu drops down from the name of the file showing you where the file is located. If you go down to one of the folders in that menu and release the mouse, a Finder window opens for that location.

Create a disk image?

To create a disk image, follow these steps:

1. Launch Disk Utility (*/Application/Utilities*).

2. In the menu bar, select File → New → Blank Disk Image, or click on the New Image button in Disk Utility's toolbar.

3. In the Save As field, enter a name for the disk image.

4. From the Where pop-up menu, select the location where you'd like to save the disk image.

5. Set the Size, Encryption method, and Format from their respective pop-up menus.

6. Click the Create button to create the disk image; the disk image file (with a *.dmg* file extension) is saved in the location you selected, and the image itself is mounted on your desktop.

7. Double-click on the disk image to open its Finder window.

8. Drag and drop the items you would like included in the disk image into the image's Finder window; a copy of the file is placed in the open disk image.

9. When you're finished, eject the disk image by either clicking the Eject icon next to its name in the Finder's Sidebar or selecting the disk image and selecting File → Eject *image_name* (⌘-E) to complete the process.

To create a disk image from an actual disk, such as your hard drive or a CD, follow these steps:

1. Launch Disk Utility (*/Application/Utilities*).

2. In the left side of Disk Utility's window, select the disk you'd like to create an image of.

3. In the menu bar, select File → New → Disk Image from *disk name*.

4. In the Save As field, enter a name for the image you want to create.

5. From the Where pop-up menu, select the location where you'd like to save the disk image.

6. Select the Image Format and Encryption Type from their respective pop-up menus.

7. Click the Create button to create the disk image.

To create a disk image from a folder so you can burn and back it up to a CD:

1. Launch Disk Utility (*/Applications/Utilities*).

2. In the menu bar, select File → New → Disk Image from Folder.

3. The "Select Folder to Image" window pops open; use this window just as you would a Finder window and select the folder you want to image; click the Image button.

4. The name of the folder appears in the Save As field; if you want to change this, enter a new name for the image you want to create.

5. From the Where pop-up menu, select the location where you'd like to save the disk image.

6. Select the Image Format and Encryption Type from their respective pop-up menus.

7. Click the Save button to create the disk image.

Burn a disk image to CD?

To burn a disk image you've created (see the previous descriptions):

1. Launch Disk Utility (*/Applications/Utilities*).

2. In the left pane of Disk Utility's window, select the disk image you want to burn to disc.

3. In the toolbar, click the Burn button.

4. Insert a blank CD.

5. Click Burn.

Display the contents of a shared folder on another volume in my network?

Finder → *volume* → *folder*.

From your home directory in the Terminal:

```
MacTiger:~ chuck$ ls -la /Volumes/volume/folder
```

Quickly create a directory and a set of numbered directories (such as for chapters in a book)?

```
MacTiger:~ chuck$ mkdir -p NewBook/{ch{01,02,03,04,05}}
MacTiger:~ chuck$ ls -F NewBook
ch01/ ch02/ ch03/ ch04/ ch05/
```

Try doing this in the Finder—you can't! The command *ls -F NewBook* is used to list the directories within the *NewBook* directory; it shows us that five separate subdirectories have been created.

Move a file to the Trash from the Finder?

Select the file and press ⌘-Delete.

Move a file to the Trash from the Terminal?

```
MacTiger:~/Desktop chuck$ mv myFile.txt ~/.Trash
```

Quickly delete a directory (and its subdirectories) without sending it to the Trash?
> MacTiger:~ chuck$ **rm -rf work**

Make the Trash stop asking me if I'm sure I want to delete every file?
> Finder → Preferences → Advanced → uncheck the option next to "Show warning before emptying the Trash."

Empty the Trash of locked items?
> Shift-Option-⌘-Delete. The addition of the Option key forces the deletion of Trash contents.

Give a file or folder a custom icon?
> Open an image file and copy it with ⌘-C. Select the icon → File → Get Info (or ⌘-I). Select the file icon in the General section and then paste in (⌘-V) the new image.

NOTE

The proper image size for an icon is 128×128 pixels.

Fonts and Font Management

Use the following options for fonts and font management:

Share fonts with other users on my system?
> If you're the administrator, move the font you'd like to share from your */Users/username/Library/Fonts* directory to */Library/Fonts*.

Where can I store new fonts I've purchased or downloaded from the Internet?
> Save them to */Users/username/Library/Fonts* for your personal use, or save them to */Library/Fonts* to allow everyone on the system access to them.

Why aren't my bitmap fonts working?
> Mac OS X doesn't support bitmapped fonts; it supports only TrueType, OpenType, and PostScript Level 1 fonts.

What does the .dfont extension on some of my Mac OS X fonts mean?

The extension stands for Data Fork TrueType Font. Basically, it just tells you the font is a TrueType font.

Turn off font antialiasing?

You can't, but you can adjust the minimum font size so that it's affected by font smoothing in System Preferences → Appearance → "Turn off text smoothing for font sizes X and smaller" (8 points is the default setting).

Create a Font Collection?

Launch the Font Book application (*/Applications*) and follow these steps:

1. Select File → New Collection (⌘-N) from the menu bar.

2. A new collection named New-0 (or some other number) appears in the Collection column; type in a different name (such as BookFonts) and press Return.

3. In the Collection column, click on All Fonts to see a list of the installed fonts in the Font column.

4. Drag the fonts you want from the Font column and drop them onto the name of the collection you've created.

NOTE

You can ⌘-click on the font names to select multiple fonts at one time before dragging them to your Font Collection.

Where are my Font Collections stored?

/Users/username/Library/FontCollections. If you want to share a collection with another user, place a copy of the collection in the Shared folder. All Font Collections have a *.collection* file extension.

Spotlight and Searching for Files

The following will help you search for and locate files:

Find a file if I don't know its name?

Use ⌘-Space to open Spotlight's search field; enter a keyword in the field.

Finder → enter a keyword in the toolbar search field.

Finder → File → Find (⌘-F).

Find a file if I can't remember where I saved it?

Hit ⌘-Space to open Spotlight's search field → enter the name of the file → select the file in the list of items Spotlight finds; the file opens in its default application.

Change the shortcut key for opening Spotlight's search field?

System Preferences → Spotlight → Spotlight menu keyboard shortcut → click the pop-up menu to select one of the F keys (F1–F12) or type in your own shortcut (for example Control-⌘-Space, which appears in the menu as ⌘^ Space).

Change the order in which Spotlight displays its search results?

System Preferences → Spotlight → Search Results → select and drag categories in the order you prefer; for example, select and drag Documents to the top of the list.

Use Spotlight to display a slideshow of the images in my iPhoto Library?

Option-⌘-Space → enter *.jpg* or *.jpeg* in the search field → in the right column under Where, select Home → to the left, in the blue Images bar, click the Play button; your screen goes black and the JPEG images in your Home folder appear as a slideshow. (Hit the Escape key to stop the slideshow.)

Display metadata for an image I shot with my digital camera?

Use Spotlight to find the file you're looking for (see previous tasks) → click the "i" icon to the right of the filename. A larger view of the image appears, displaying all sorts of information about the image, including the camera model, exposure time, and the date and time the image was taken, to name a few.

Stop Spotlight from searching through my music files?

System Preferences → Spotlight → Privacy → click the Add (+) button → select your Music folder → click Choose to add your Music folder to the list.

Build the locate database in a way that allows me to search for files by name using the Terminal?

Use the *locate* command in the Terminal. However, you must first update the *locate* database as follows:

```
MacTiger:~ chuck$ cd /usr/libexec
MacTiger:/usr/libexec chuck$ sudo ./locate.updatedb
```

If you haven't built the *locate* database yet, this command could take a few minutes to run; after it runs, you are returned to the command line.

NOTE

The *locate.updatedb* command is executed weekly by default, as noted in the */etc/weekly* file. However, you might want to issue this command yourself shortly after installing Mac OS X Tiger.

Now you can use the *locate* command:

```
MacTiger:/usr/libexec chuck$ locate temp98.doc
/Users/chuck/Books/Templates/temp98.doc
MacTiger:/usr/libexec chuck$
```

In this example I used *locate* to search for the file *temp98.doc*; in return, the command tells me the name of the directory in which the file is located.

Obtaining Information About the System

Use the following if you need to obtain system information:

Find out how much disk space I have left?

Launch the Finder and look in the thin bar just below the toolbar. You will see something that says how many items are in that directory and how much space is available on your hard drive.

Issue the *df -H* command in the Terminal, as shown in Figure 42. This shows the amount of space Used and Avail(able) for each mounted drive or partition. On this system, the */dev/disk0s12* filesystem is that of Mac OS X Tiger, which is at 86% capacity. Note that the numbers shown in the Used and Avail columns are listed in human-readable form (G for gigabytes, M for megabytes, K for kilobytes).

```
000                    Terminal — bash — 80x12
MacChuckTiger:~ chuck$ df -H
Filesystem              Size    Used    Avail  Capacity  Mounted on
/dev/disk0s12           5.2G    4.5G    728M   86%       /
devfs                   104K    104K    0B     100%      /dev
fdesc                   1.0K    1.0K    0B     100%      /dev
<volfs>                 524K    524K    0B     100%      /.vol
/dev/disk0s10           25G     20G     4.7G   81%       /Volumes/Panther
automount -nsl [188]    0B      0B      0B     100%      /Network
automount -fstab [192]  0B      0B      0B     100%      /automount/Servers
automount -static [192] 0B      0B      0B     100%      /automount/static
MacChuckTiger:~ chuck$
```

Figure 42. Using df -H to display the available disk space on your Mac

Find out how much memory I have?

 → About This Mac.

Find out what version of Mac OS X I'm running?

 → About This Mac.

 → About This Mac; click on the version number (e.g., 10.4) to reveal the build number (e.g., 8A428).

System Profiler (*/Applications/Utilities*) → Contents → select Software to see the exact build of Mac OS X.

Find out what processor my Mac has?

 → About This Mac.

System Profiler (*/Applications/Utilities*) → Contents → select Hardware.

Find out what type of cache I have and how big is it?
System Profiler (*/Applications/Utilities*) → Contents → select Hardware → look for L2 and/or L3 Cache items, to the right.

Find out whether a drive is formatted with HFS?
Disk Utility (*/Applications/Utilities*) → select the drive or partition in the left column → click on the Info button → the File System type should read Mac OS Extended (Journaled).

Find out what programs (or processes) are running?
Activity Monitor (*/Applications/Utilities*).

From the command line, use the *ps -aux* command.

From the command line, use the *top* command.

Display the status of the computer's used and free memory?
Issuing the *top* command in the Terminal displays something similar to what's shown in Figure 43.

The *top* command gives you a real-time view of the processes running on your system, as well as processor and memory usage. To see how much memory is available to you, look at the end of the PhysMem line; in this case, the system is using 532 megabytes (532M) of RAM and has 235 megabytes (235M) free. To stop the *top* command from running, hit Control-C or ⌘-., which cancel the process.

View the hardware connected to my system?
System Profiler (*/Applications/Utilities*). This information can be found in the Hardware section.

Create a profile of my Mac with System Profiler?
If you need to call AppleCare for assistance, it's always good to have a recent copy of your system profile on hand. Your system profile, which is created with System Profiler (*/Applications/Utilities*), provides a detailed list of

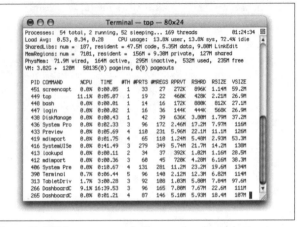

Figure 43. Unix's top command tells you a lot about what's going on with your system.

information about your Mac's hardware configuration (type of hard drive, amount of RAM, and so on), as well as the applications, extensions, and other important system logs for your computer. To create a profile of your Mac, follow these steps:

1. In the Finder, go to your Applications → Utilities folder (or use the keyboard shortcut Shift-⌘-U to quickly open the Utilities folder in the Finder).

2. Launch the System Profiler.

3. From the File menu, select Save.

4. In the field at the top of the sheet that appears, give your system profile a name, such as *chucktoporek_sysprofile*.

5. In the Where pop-up, the location of your Mac's profile is set to your Documents folder. Either leave this as it is or select another folder of your choice.

6. In the File Format pop-up, leave the type set to System Profiler 4.0 (XML).

7. Click Save.

8. Now if you ever need to file a bug with Apple or if you need a copy of your system profile to send to AppleCare, you'll have one on hand.

TIP

It's a good idea to create a copy of your system profile every week or so, just to be safe.

.Mac

Set up a .Mac account?
System Preferences → .Mac → Account → Learn More. (You must be connected to the Internet to set up a .Mac account.)

Find out how much space I have available on my iDisk?
System Preferences → .Mac → iDisk.

Require a password from other users before they can access my iDisk's Public folder?
System Preferences → .Mac → iDisk → enable the checkbox next to "Use a Password to Protect your Public Folder" and then click on the Password button to set a password.

Create a local copy of my iDisk on my hard drive so I can back it up?
System Preferences → .Mac → iDisk → enable the checkbox next to "Create a local copy of your iDisk" → select either Automatically or Manually to indicate how you want to synchronize your iDisk with your local copy.

Find out how many days are remaining on my .Mac membership before I have to renew?
System Preferences → .Mac → Account.

Mount my iDisk?

> Click the iDisk icon in the Finder's Sidebar.
>
> From the Finder's menu bar, select Go → iDisk → My iDisk.
>
> From the Finder, use the keyboard shortcut Shift-⌘-I.

Unmount my iDisk?

> Select the iDisk icon in the Finder's Sidebar and select File → Eject.
>
> Drag your iDisk's icon from the desktop to the Trash.

Synchronize data on my Mac with my .Mac account?

> System Preferences → .Mac → Sync → select the items you want to synchronize → click Sync Now.

Synchronize my Address Book contacts from my PowerBook to my G5 iMac?

> On the PowerBook, select System Preferences → .Mac → Sync → select the items you want to synchronize → click Sync Now. Go to your iMac and make sure the .Mac Account pane is set up to use your .Mac account, then go to the Advanced pane and click "Register this Computer." This registers the iMac with the .Mac synchronization server; once it's registered, go back to the Sync pane on the iMac and click Sync Now.

Safari and the Internet

Use the following settings according to your Internet, web, and email usage:

Specify where Safari saves files downloaded from the Internet?

> Safari → Preferences (⌘-,) → General → "Save downloaded files to:" → select a location in the pop-up menu.

Change Safari's default home page?

> Safari → Preferences (⌘-,) → General → "Home page" → enter a different URL in this field (for example, *http://www.macdevcenter.com*).

Enable tabbed viewing in Safari?
> Safari → Preferences (⌘-,) → Tabs → Enable Tabbed Browsing.

Set up Safari so it remembers passwords for web sites I'm required to log into?
> Safari → Preferences (⌘-,) → AutoFill → click the checkbox next to "Usernames and passwords."

Change my default RSS news reader from Safari to NetNewsWire?
> Safari → Preferences (⌘-,) → RSS → Default RSS Reader → select NetNewsWire from the pop up.

Block pop-up windows from appearing when I'm surfing the web?
> Safari → Preferences (⌘-,) → Security → click the checkbox next to "Block pop-up windows."

Set up Safari to check spelling for me when I'm using Gmail or .Mac's web-based Mail?
> Edit → Spelling → Check Spelling as You Type.

Set up Safari so it doesn't keep track of my history?
> Safari → Private Browsing (read the disclaimer window that pops up before clicking OK).

Turn on web sharing?
> System Preferences → Sharing → Services pane → enable the checkbox next to Personal Web Sharing to start this service. Enabling this service allows others to access your Sites folder (*/Users/username/Sites*) from the Internet. To learn more about Personal Web Sharing, point your default browser to */Users/username/Sites/index.html*. The address for your personal web site is *http://yourIPAddress/~yourshortusername/*.

Listen to an Internet radio station?
> Dock → iTunes → Radio. When you click the Radio option in the Source pane to the left, the right pane changes to show you a list of different music genres from

which to choose. Click the disclosure triangle next to a music type to reveal the available stations.

Use my own stylesheet for viewing web pages in Safari?
Safari → Preferences (⌘-,) → Advanced → Style Sheet → Other → locate and select the Cascading Style Sheet (CSS) you want to apply.

Create shortcuts on my desktop for web sites I visit often or email addresses I use frequently?
Open the TextEdit application, enter a URL (such as *http://www.macdevcenter.com*) or an email address (such as *chuckdude@mac.com*), then triple-click on the address to select the entire line and drag it to your desktop; this creates an icon on your desktop for whatever you drag there. When you double-click on the icon, your default web browser opens that URL, or your email client creates a new message window with the address specified by the shortcut.

Empty Safari's cache?
Safari → Empty Safari's Cache (Option-⌘-E).

Clear Safari's History file?
History → Clear History.

Mark a web page for SnapBack?
History → Mark Page for SnapBack (Option-⌘-K).

Mail.app

Everyone uses email these days, even my parents. Here are some tips to help you work with Tiger's new Mail application:

Enable junk mail filtering?
Mail → Preferences (⌘-,) → Junk Mail → turn on "Enable junk mail filtering."

Set up my mailbox to sort junk mail into a separate mailbox so spam messages don't clutter my inbox?

Mail → Preferences (⌘-,) → Junk Mail → turn on "Enable junk mail filtering." In the "When junk mail arrives" section, turn on "Move it to the Junk mailbox (Automatic)."

Get rid of the junk mail I've received?

Mailbox → Erase Junk Mail (Option-⌘-J).

Empty Mail's trash?

Mailbox → Erase Deleted Messages → In All Accounts (⌘-K).

View messages with similar subject lines as a thread?

Select the mailbox → View → Organize by Thread.

Synchronize messages with my .Mac account?

Mailbox → Synchronize Account.

Change Mail so the messages I write use plain text?

Mail → Preferences (⌘-,) → Composing → Composing: Message Format → select Plain Text from the pop-up menu.

Create Smart Mailboxes to organize my messages in Mail.app?

Regardless of whether you use your Mac at work or at home, chances are you get a lot of email every day. And what better way to help you organize your email than with Mail.app's new Smart Mailbox feature. Smart Mailboxes can be used for anything from sorting emails from your boss into a different folder than emails from your friends, to sorting your messages based on the time they were received.

For example, let's say you want to create two Smart Mailboxes, one for email messages you've received today, and another for messages you've received this week. To create these Smart Mailboxes, follow these steps:

1. Launch Mail.app by clicking its icon in the Dock or by double-clicking its icon in the Finder.

2. From the Mailbox menu, select the New Smart Mailbox item.

3. In the Smart Mailbox Name field, type in "Today's Email".

4. Change the From pop-up to Date Received, and leave the second pop-up set to "is today."

5. Click OK.

This creates a Smart Mailbox that, when selected, only displays the Inbox messages that came in today. Now create another Smart Mailbox for email received this week:

1. From the Mailbox menu, select the New Smart Mailbox item.

2. In the Smart Mailbox Name field, type in "This Week".

3. Change the From pop-up to Date Received.

4. Change the second pop-up from "is today" to "is this week."

5. Click OK.

The possibilities are limitless, so use your imagination and create Smart Mailboxes to automatically sort and sift your messages to your heart's content!

Modems and Dial-Up Networking

Use the following options to configure your modem and dial-up networking:

Configure a modem for dialing into my ISP?
Go to System Preferences → Network, and follow these steps:

1. Select New Location from the Location pull-down menu. Enter a name for the new location (for example, My ISP) and click OK.

2. Select Internal Modem from the Show pull-down menu.

3. Fill in the blanks on the PPP panel.

4. In the TCP/IP panel, select Using PPP from the Configure IPv4 pull-down menu.

5. Select your modem type from the Modem panel.

6. Click the Apply Now button.

Show the modem status in the menu bar?
   System Preferences → Network → select Internal Modem from the Show pull-down menu → Modem pane → click on the checkbox next to "Show modem status in menu bar."

Make sure my modem is working?
   Applications → Internet Connect.

Set my computer to wake up from sleep mode when the modem rings?
   System Preferences → Energy Saver → Options → Wake Options; turn on "Wake when the modem detects a ring."

Find out the speed of my dial-up connection?
   Applications → Internet Connect. The bottom section of the window tells you the speed of your connection.

Disable call waiting on my phone when using the modem?
   System Preferences → Network → PPP → add "*70," before the beginning of the telephone number you're dialing (e.g., *70, 1-503-555-1212).

Where are my modem configuration files stored?
   /Library/Modem Scripts

Specify how many times my modem will redial if it detects a busy signal?
   System Preferences → Network → Show → Internal Modem → PPP panel → PPP Options → Session Options → Redial if busy → Redial x times.

Networking

The following settings aid with networking settings:

Find the media access control (MAC) address for my Ethernet card?

> System Preferences → Network → Show → Built-in Ethernet → Ethernet pane → Ethernet ID.

Configure my system to connect to an Ethernet network?

> Go to System Preferences → Network and follow these steps:

> 1. Select New Location from the Location pull-down menu. Enter a name for the new location (for example, "Work") and click OK.

> 2. Select Built-in Ethernet from the Show pull-down menu.

> 3. From the Configure pull-down menu in the TCP/IP panel, select Using DHCP if your IP address is assigned dynamically, or Manually if your machine has a fixed IP address. (In most cases, particularly if you have a broadband Internet connection at home, your IP address is assigned via DHCP.)

> 4. If you're on an AppleTalk network, select the Make AppleTalk Active option in the AppleTalk panel and select your Zone (if any).

> 5. Click Apply Now.

> Repeat as necessary to add other network configurations. For example, you could create Location settings for your Home AirPort Network or Home Ethernet Network, depending on whether you have a wireless or wired network at home.

Configure my system to connect to a VPN?

> Here's how to set up your Mac OS X system for connecting to a VPN:

> 1. Launch Internet Connect (*/Applications*).

2. Click the VPN icon (the one that looks like a pad-lock) in the toolbar.

3. Select the type of VPN you're going to connect to, either "L2TP over IPSec" or "PPTP"; click Continue.

4. In the Configuration popup, select Edit Configurations; a sheet appears giving you options for configuring your VPN connection's settings.

5. In the Description field, assign a name to your VPN connection, such as "Work VPN."

6. Tab to the Server Address field and enter the address to your VPN server (for example, *vpn.oreilly.com*).

7. Tab to the Account Name field and enter your account name (ask your system administrator for this). If your VPN is on a Windows-based server, enter the domain as well; for example, *domain\chuck*.

8. Tab to the User Authentication field and either enter your Password in the field or select one of the other two options (RSA SecurID or Certificate).

9. In the Encryption pop-up, select the encryption type for your VPN connection (typically, leaving this set to "Automatic (128 bit or 40 bit)" should suffice).

10. If you use your VPN to connect to work for checking email, you should consider turning on the "Enable VPN on demand" feature. When you do, the "VPN on Demand Domains" window pops open and you can add domains which, if a connection attempt is made, automatically start the VPN connection for you. This is particularly helpful at times when you forget to start the VPN before launching Mail.

11. Click OK to accept the VPN configuration settings.

12. In Internet Connect's window, turn on the "Show VPN status in menu bar" item. This places a menu extra in the menu bar, which you can use to connect to your VPN. Once you are connected, the menu

extra also tells you how long you've been connected to the server.

13. Click Connect to connect to your VPN server. (The Status indicator in this window tells you whether you're connected and shows the IP address assigned to your machine by the server.)

When you want to connect to the VPN in the future, follow these steps:

1. Go to the menu bar and click the VPN menu extra (it looks like a black rectangle, with an open white gap on the left edge).

2. Move the mouse down and select Connect to make your connection.

NOTE

If you have more than one VPN you can connect to, you'll see the other server names listed in this menu. You'll need to select the VPN you want to connect to, click on the VPN menu extra again, and select Connect to make the connection.

When you've completed the work you needed to do over the VPN, go back to the VPN menu extra and select Disconnect.

Change my computer's name from my full name to something else?

System Preferences → Sharing; enter the new name in the Computer Name text box. Your computer's name, which is also used for Bonjour networking, has a *.local* extension; for example, *MacTiger.local*.

Find out the speed of my network connection?

Network Utility (*/Applications/Utilities*) → Info panel; look next to Link Speed in the Interface Information section.

Find out what's taking a site so long to respond?

Network Utility (*/Applications/Utilities*) → Ping panel → enter the network address for the location (e.g., *http://www.macdevcenter.com* or *10.0.2.1*).

Use the *ping* command along with a hostname (such as a web site's URL, minus the *http://* prefix) in the Terminal:

```
MacTiger:~ chuck$ ping www.macdevcenter.com
```

Trace the route taken to connect to a web page?

Network Utility (*/Applications/Utilities*) → Traceroute panel → enter the hostname for the location.

Use the *traceroute* command along with a hostname in the Terminal:

```
MacTiger:~ chuck$ traceroute www.macdevcenter.com
```

Allow others access to my computer so they can retrieve files I make available to them?

System Preferences → Sharing → Services → click "Personal File Sharing" → click the Start button. This turns on file sharing, which gives others access to your Public folder (*/Users/username/Public*). The Public folder is read-only, which means that other people can only view or copy files in that folder; they cannot save files to that folder.

Allow my coworkers to place files on my computer without giving them access to the rest of my system?

With Personal File Sharing turned on (see previous item), other users can place files, folders, or even applications in your Drop Box, located within the Public folder (*/Users/username/Public/Drop Box*).

View what's inside someone else's iDisk Public folder?

Go → Connect to Server. At the bottom of the dialog box, type *http://idisk.mac.com/membername/Public*. Click Connect or press Return; the Public iDisk image mounts on your desktop.

Connect to a networked drive?

Go → Connect to Server (⌘-K).

If the server to which you want to connect is part of your local area network (LAN), click on the Local icon in the left pane and select the server name to the right. If the server to which you want to connect is part of your local AppleTalk network, click the AppleTalk Network icon in the left pane and select the server or computer name to the right.

Connect to a Windows server?

If you need to connect to a Windows server, you must specify the address in the text box as follows:

```
smb://hostname/sharename
```

After clicking the Connect button, you are asked to supply the domain to which you wish to connect and your username and password.

You can speed up this process by supplying the domain and your username, as follows:

```
smb://domain;username@hostname/sharename
```

where *domain* is the NT domain name, *username* is the name you use to connect to that *domain*, and *hostname* and *sharename* are the server name and shared directory that you have or want access to. For example:

    smb://seb01;chuck@rosetta.east.ora.com/work

Now when you click the Connect button, all you need to do is enter your password (if one is required), and the networked drive mounts on your desktop.

NOTE

Before pressing the Connect button, press the button with a plus sign (+) to add the server to your list of Favorites. This saves you time in the future if you frequently need to connect to the same drive because you won't have to enter its address again.

AirPort and Wireless Networking

Here are some useful tips for working with a wireless system:

Add the AirPort menu extra to the menu bar?
> System Preferences → Network → Show → AirPort → AirPort → enable "Show AirPort status in menu bar."

Find the MAC address for my AirPort card?
> System Preferences → Network → Show → AirPort → AirPort → AirPort ID.

Quickly switch to an AirPort network after disconnecting the Ethernet cable from my iBook?
> System Preferences → Network → Show → Network Port Configurations. Click the checkboxes next to the network ports you want to enable and drag the ports in the list to place them in the order in which you're most likely to connect to them. (Setting the Location pop-up to Automatic should do the trick for you, but it doesn't always work.)

Share my modem or Ethernet connection with other AirPort-equipped Macs?

System Preferences → Sharing → Internet → in the "To computers using" listbox, turn on AirPort → click the Start button to turn on Internet sharing.

Find out why my AirPort connection seems so sluggish?

For this, you'll need to download Apple's AirPort Management Tools:

1. Go to *http://www.apple.com/support/airport/* and look to the right under Additional Resources for a link to download the AirPort Management Tools.

2. Click the link to download this disk image to your Mac.

3. Once the disk image mounts on your system, drag the AirPort Client Monitor and AirPort Management Utility applications to your Utilities folder (*/Applications/Utilities*); this keeps all of the AirPort utilities together in one place.

4. Launch the AirPort Client Monitor by double-clicking its icon.

If the bars are low in the Signal and Transmit Rate sections, chances are your AirPort connection is encountering some interference. The higher the bars, the better your connection. Try moving your AirPort or Mac around the room to see if your signal improves.

Share a USB printer over an AirPort network?

If you have an AirPort Extreme or AirPort Express Base Station, all you need to do is connect the USB cord to the Base Station, and the printer automatically becomes available to computers on the network.

If the printer is directly connected to your Mac, you'll need to enable Printer Sharing. For this, go to System Preferences → Sharing → Services → click the checkbox next to Printer Sharing.

Printer Configuration and Printing

Use the following options for printer configuration and printing:

Configure a printer?

Launch Printer Setup Utility (*/Applications/Utilities*) and either click on the Add button in the Printer List window or select Printer → Add Printer from the menu bar. Using the pull-down menu, select the type of printer connection (AppleTalk, IP Printing, Open Directory, Bonjour, USB, or Windows):

- If you selected AppleTalk, select the zone (if any) using the second pull-down menu, choose the printer in the lower pane and then click the Add button.

- If you selected IP Printing, you'll need to know and fill in the IP address of the printer; select the printer model and then click the Add button.

- If you selected Open Directory, you can choose a printer listed in the NetInfo Network. Select the printer name and then click the Add button.

- If you selected Bonjour, USB, or Windows, choose the name of the printer and the printer model, and then click the Add button.

View the jobs in the print queue?

Launch the Printer Setup Utility → double-click on the name of the printer to see the print queue.

Cancel a print job?

Launch the Printer Setup Utility → double-click on the printer name → click on the name of the print job → click the Delete button.

Halt a print job?

Launch the Printer Setup Utility → double-click on the printer name → click on the name of the print job → click on the Hold button. (Click on the Resume button to start the job where it left off.)

Share my printer with another user?
System Preferences → Sharing → Services → turn on the checkbox next to Printer Sharing.

Maintenance and Troubleshooting

The following settings deal with maintenance and trouble-shooting issues:

Force quit an application that's stuck?
Option-⌘-Escape opens a window that shows all the running applications. Select the troublesome application and click the Force Quit button.

Option-click the application's icon in the Dock. In the contextual menu that appears, select the Force Quit option.

Activity Monitor (*/Applications/Utilities*) → select the process causing the problem → Processes → Quit Process.

Restart my system if it's completely frozen?
Hold down the Shift-Option-⌘ keys and press the Power-On button.

Fix a disk that won't mount?
Disk Utility (*/Applications/Utilities*) → select the disk that won't mount → First Aid.

Return my system to functionality if it has frozen after launching an application?
Follow these steps:

1. Do a hard restart of your system: Control-⌘-Power-On (or Eject).

2. Log back into your system.

3. Launch the Terminal (*/Applications/Utilities*).

4. Enter the following command and hit Return:

   ```
   MacTiger:~ chuck$ sudo shutdown -h now
   ```

This forces an automatic shutdown of your system.

5. Press the Power-On button on your Mac and hold down ⌘-S during startup to boot your Mac into single-user mode. Your screen will go black and you'll be given a text prompt.

6. At the prompt, enter the following command:

```
sh-2.05a# fsck -f
```

The *fsck* command performs a filesystem check and reports back its findings:

```
bootstrap_look_up( ) failed (ip/send) invalid
destination port
bootstrap_look_up( ) failed (ip/send) invalid
destination port
bootstrap_look_up( ) failed (ip/send) invalid
destination port
** /dev/rdisk0s2
** Root file system
** Checking HFS Plus volume.
** Checking Extents Overflow file.
** Checking Catalog file.
** Checking multi-linked files.
** Checking Catalog hierarchy.
** Checking volume bitmap.
** Checking volume information.
** The volume MacTiger appears to be OK.
sh-2.05a#
```

If *fsck -f* reports that the disk has been modified, you'll need to run the command again until the filesystem checks out to be OK.

7. If everything within your filesystem is fine, enter *reboot* at the command prompt and hit Return to reboot your system.

Partition a new hard drive?

Applications → Utilities → Disk Utility → select the new drive → Partition.

Erase a CD-RW disc or hard drive?

Disk Utility (*/Applications/Utilities*) → select the CD or disk → Erase.

Create a redundant array of independent disks (RAID) for my system?

Disk Utility (*/Applications/Utilities*) → select the drives → RAID.

Access command-line mode and bypass Aqua?

There are two ways you can access the command-line interface:

- Hold down ⌘-S when starting up the system; this is known as *single-user mode*.
- At the login window, type *>console* as the username, enter your password, and click on the Login button. This is known as multi-user mode and is just like being in the Terminal, except that your entire screen is the Terminal.

When you've finished diagnosing your system, type *shutdown -r now* and press Return to reboot your system into Aqua.

Rebuild Classic's desktop?

System Preferences → Classic → Advanced panel. There is no need to rebuild Mac OS X's desktop, so holding down the Option-⌘ keys at startup is futile.

All the icons on my system look funny. Is there an easy way to fix this problem?

Even though Mac OS X is more reliable than earlier versions of the Mac OS, icons and such can still go haywire. The quick fix for this problem is to delete the three LS files (*LSApplications*, *LSClaimedTypes*, and *LSSchemes*) in *~/Library/Preferences*.

There is a question mark icon in the Dock. What is this?

A question mark icon in the Dock or in one of the toolbars means that the application, folder, or file that the original icon related to has been deleted from your system. Just drag the question mark icon away from the Dock or toolbar to make it disappear.

I have a dual-processor Power Mac G5. Can I see how effi-
ciently the processors are distributing the workload?

Activity Monitor (*/Applications/Utilities*) → CPU; each
processor has its own meter bar.

View a log of software updates?

System Preferences → Software Update → Show Log.

How do I connect an external monitor or projector to my
PowerBook without restarting it?

Select → Sleep to put your laptop to sleep, plug in and
turn on the display, and then hit the Escape key to wake
your system and the display. You can then use the Displays preference panel (System Preferences → Displays)
to turn display mirroring on or off as needed.

PART VIII

Special Characters

Included with Mac OS X is the Keyboard Viewer application, which is a keyboard widget that allows you to see which character is created by applying the Shift, Option, or Shift-Option keys to any key on the keyboard. To enable Keyboard Viewer, go to System Preferences → International → Input Menu and select the checkbox next to Keyboard Viewer. The Input menu appears in the menu bar; to launch the Keyboard Viewer, simply select this item from the Input menu.

While this application might seem useful, it can be a hassle to launch another app just to create one character and copy and paste it into another program. Fortunately, the Mac OS is able (through one of its least-known and most infrequently used features) to give you the same functionality within any application, making Keyboard Viewer unnecessary if you know what you're doing.

Table 11 lists the special characters. Keep in mind that this doesn't work for all font types, and some fonts, such as Symbol, Wingdings, and Zapf Dingbats, create an entirely different set of characters or symbols. For example, to create the symbol for the Command key (⌘), you would need to switch the font to Wingdings and type a lowercase "z".

Table 11. Special characters and their key mappings

Normal	Shift	Option	Shift-Option
1	!	¡	⁄
2	@	™	€

Table 11. Special characters and their key mappings (continued)

Normal	Shift	Option	Shift-Option
3	#	£	‹
4	$	¢	›
5	%	∞	fi
6	^	§	fl
7	&	¶	‡
8	*	•	°
9	(	ª	·
0	)	º	‚
`	~	Grave (`)[a]	‘
- (hyphen)	_ (underscore)	– (en-dash)	— (em-dash)
=	+	≠	±
[	{	"	"
]	}	'	'
\	|	«	»
;	:	…	Ú
'	"	æ	Æ
,	<	≤	¯
.	>	≥	˘
/	?	÷	¿
a	A	å	Å
b	B	∫	ı
c	C	ç	Ç
d	D	∂	Î
e	E	Acute (´)[a]	´
f	F	ƒ	Ï
g	G	©	˝
h	H	˙	Ó
i	I	Circumflex (ˆ)[a]	ˆ

Table 11. Special characters and their key mappings (continued)

Normal	Shift	Option	Shift-Option
j	J	Δ	Ô
k	K	°	<img_apple>
l	L	¬	Ò
m	M	μ	Â
n	N	Tilde (˜)[a]	˜
o	O	ø	Ø
p	P	π	Π
q	Q	œ	Œ
r	R	®	‰
s	S	ß	Í
t	T	†	ˇ
u	U	Umlaut (¨)[a]	¨
v	V	√	◊
w	W	Σ	„
x	X	≈	˛
y	Y	¥	Á
z	Z	Ω	˒

[a] To apply this accent, you must press another key after invoking the Option-key command. See Table 12.

One thing you might have noticed in Table 12 is that when the Option key is used with certain letters, it doesn't necessarily create a special character right away; you need to press another character key to apply the accent. When used with the ` (backtick), E, I, N, and U characters, the Option key creates the accented characters shown in Table 12.

Table 12. Option-key commands for creating accented characters

Key	Option-`	Option-E	Option-I	Option-N	Option-U
a	à	á	â	Ã	ä
Shift-A	À	Á	Â	Ã	Ä

Table 12. Option-key commands for creating accented characters

Key	Option-`	Option-E	Option-I	Option-N	Option-U
e	è	é	ê	~e	ë
Shift-E	È	É	Ê	~E	Ë
i	ì	í	î	~i	ï
Shift-I	Ì	Í	Î	~I	Ï
o	ò	ó	ô	Õ	ö
Shift-O	Ò	Ó	Ô	Õ	Ö
u	ù	ú	Û	~u	ü
Shift-U	Ù	Ú	û	~U	Ü

For example, to create the acute-accented "e"s in the word "résumé," you would type Option-E and then press the E key. If you want an uppercase acute-accented "E" (É), press Option-E and then Shift-E. Try this out with various characters in different fonts to see what sort of characters you can create.

Index

We'd like to hear your suggestions for improving our indexes. Send email to
index@oreilly.com.

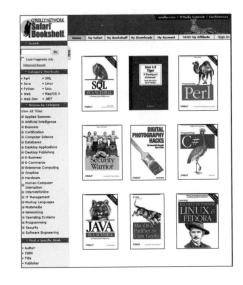

Related Titles Available from O'Reilly

Macintosh

AppleScript: The Definitive Guide

Appleworks 6: The Missing Manual

The Best of the Joy of Tech

FileMaker Pro 7: The Missing Manual

GarageBand: The Missing Manual

iLife '04: The Missing Manual

iMovie 4 and iDVD: The Missing Manual

iPhoto 4: The Missing Manual

iPod & iTunes: The Missing Manual, *2nd Edition*

Mac OS X Panther in a Nutshell

Mac OS X Panther Pocket Guide

Mac OS X Panther Power User

Mac OS X: The Missing Manual, Panther Edition

Mac OS X Unwired

Macintosh Troubleshooting Pocket Guide

Modding Mac OS X

Office X for the Macintosh: The Missing Manual

Revolutionaries in The Valley: Their Incredible Stories of How the Mac was Made

Running Mac OS X Panther

Mac Developers

Building Cocoa Applications: A Step-By-Step Guide

Cocoa in a Nutshell

Learning Carbon

Learning Cocoa with Objective-C, *2nd Edition*

Learning Unix for Mac OS X Panther

Mac OS X for Java Geeks

Mac OS X Hacks

Mac OS X Panther Hacks

Mac OS X Panther for Unix Geeks

Managing & Using Mac OS X Server

Objective-C Pocket Reference

RealBasic: The Definitive Guide, *2nd Edition*

O'REILLY®

Our books are available at most retail and online bookstores.
To order direct: 1-800-998-9938 • *order@oreilly.com* • *www.oreilly.com*
Online editions of most O'Reilly titles are available at *safari.oreilly.com*